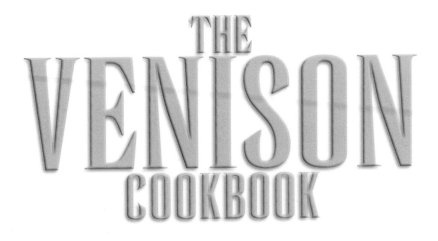

THE VENISON COOKBOOK

Venison Dishes from Fast to Fancy

KATE FIDUCCIA

Skyhorse Publishing

First Paperback Edition 2018

Skyhorse Publishing books may be purchased in bulk at special discounts for sales promotion, corporate gifts, fund-raising, or educational purposes. Special editions can also be created to specifications. For details, contact the Special Sales Department, Skyhorse Publishing, 307 West 36th Street, 11th Floor, New York, NY 10018 or info@skyhorsepublishing.com.

Skyhorse® and Skyhorse Publishing® are registered trademarks of Skyhorse Publishing, Inc.®, a Delaware corporation.

www.skyhorsepublishing.com

10 9 8 7 6 5 4 3

Library of Congress Cataloging-in-Publication Data is available on file.

Paperback ISBN: 978-1-5107-3725-9
Hardcover ISBN: 978-1-61608-456-1
Ebook ISBN: 978-1-6287-3213-9

Printed in China

Introduction

I often muse about the adage, "The way to a man's heart is through his stomach." That expression must stem from the days when a cave woman prepared food for the man, who was the primary hunter in the family. While it's no longer a politically correct sentiment, it's still quite valid. Food can be seductive and romantic to either gender.

Over the centuries, some of us were fortunate enough to retain a "gathering" gene—the instinct to hunt. In modern days, being able to enjoy the privilege of going afield to hunt for your meal is taking the act of cooking to the next level and is an experience only another hunter can appreciate.

Today, venison meat is quite the rage even for non-hunters. It is touted to be a healthy, low-fat alternative to traditional domestic meat such as beef, lamb, pork and even veal. Each year, more and more deer and elk farms are cropping up that sell their domestically raised venison and some imported venison through mail-order catalogs. (See the Appendix on page 122 for a source list.)

No matter how you acquire your venison, this cookbook will give you a plethora of easy-to-prepare, practical and delicious venison recipes. All the recipes originate from experiences I have had as an outdoor communicator. My career began in 1983, when I started co-hosting my husband's television program, *Woods N' Water*. Since then, Peter and I have hunted a wide variety of wild-game animals across North America and shared our hunting experiences and knowledge with viewers.

In 1994, I wrote a chapter on wild-game cooking in Peter's book *Whitetail Strategies*. I received such a huge response, we decided to produce a wild-game cooking segment on our show called "Going Wild in Kate's Kitchen," filmed right in my own kitchen. Viewers wrote in to say that while they enjoyed the hunting stories, the cooking segments were the favorite of both men and women. Many said that "Going Wild in Kate's Kitchen" had favorably changed a spouse's or family member's opinion of hunting; some even reported that the cooking segments had persuaded a wife, daughter or son to try hunting. This gave me more encouragement to write a cookbook.

Another factor that pushed me to write this book was the fabulous meals Peter and I have enjoyed at the outfitters we've visited over the years. Some of the talented cooks who prepared these feasts weren't formally schooled in cooking, but believe me, the wild-game meals they prepared were just as delicious as those of the classically trained chefs. There is a knack to cooking wild game, and these folks have fine-tuned their techniques to turn out the best in wild-game and venison cuisine. In this book, I've shared a number of recipes from these wonderful places. I'm quite sure that if they're crowd pleasers at camp, they'll be a hit with your family as well!

One of the main themes of this book is to have fun with the recipes, experiment, and most importantly, enjoy. Whether you are a "seasoned" chef (I had to use that play on words somewhere in this book) who has prepared and cooked venison for many years, or a novice, I hope this volume will be a valued addition to your cookbook collection.

Table of Contents

Working with Venison

The term venison is broadly defined as the meat from any game animal, including not only the deer and its relatives, but also bear, antelope, wild boar, peccary and more. For the purposes of this cookbook, however, venison refers to the more customary group of deer, elk, caribou and moose meat.

One of the prime benefits of venison is its low fat content. With only 3.6 grams of fat in a 4-ounce piece of meat*, venison is one of the healthiest meats available today. In addition, wild venison has not been injected with preservatives, hormones, antibiotics or other substances associated with certain health risks.

How do deer, elk, caribou and moose venison differ from one another? Before I answer that question, I'd like to mention a factor that has a huge effect on the taste of any game meat, and that is proper field-dressing and butchering (see pages 115-119 for more information on field care). Whether the animal ate luscious farm-country corn, scrappy wild grasses from the plains, or berries and lichens from the tundra, if the downed animal was left to sit afield for a day or even several hours before being field-dressed, the meat will not be at its prime. With that said, I will tell you that I and many other wild-game cooks feel that moose is one of the finer venisons. However, elk ranks close to the top as well, and there can be quite a heated debate about which meat is better. Some die-hard venison aficionados even swear that whitetail venison is the best-tasting of all. I'll let you be the judge.

The most significant difference between venison from various species is the size of the cuts. For example, a loin medallion from a deer will be 2 to 4 inches across, while one from a moose averages 5 to 8 inches across. Many venison cuts resemble comparable cuts of veal in size; in color and texture, however, they resemble beef.

Over the years, one of the questions I have been asked most frequently is, "Is there a secret to cooking venison?" My answer is always the same: "No, but there are some important tips—in and out of the kitchen—that will help you serve better-tasting wild game." Here are my number-one tips; follow them and you'll be able to prepare venison that your family and guests will have a hard time distinguishing from the tastiest cuts of beef or veal.

To save space in my freezer, I prefer to bone as much meat as possible. The only cuts that aren't boned are ribs and the rack of venison. Boned cuts make attractive table fare and are easy to carve.

Most roasts come from the top round and bottom round portions of the hindquarters. If a boneless portion is too flat to cook as a roast, turn it into a rolled roast. Roll with the grain of the meat so that when the roast is carved, slices will be across the grain. Keep the ends as even as possible. Use strong kitchen string to tie the roast, tying the ends first and spacing the ties evenly, about one inch apart. The ties should be tight enough to eliminate pockets where juices can collect and spoilage can start.

When cooking a venison roast with dry heat, you'll need to add additional fat to keep it moist. Since larding—threading strips of fat into the interior of the roast with the aid of a special needle—is not commonplace anymore, simply wrap bacon or pork fat around the roast.

Always remember that venison should not be overcooked. I find that venison is most tasty when rare (130° to 135°F). If it is cooked to 150°F, it will be medium-well, and this is starting to get overcooked in my opinion. It is not often that you find a large cut of well-done venison that is tasty. When cooking a large piece of venison like a roast, a quality meat thermometer is a crucial piece of equipment.

Steaks are usually cut from the top sirloin, top round and sirloin butt sections; medallions and kabobs often come from the loin and tenderloin. They should be cut about an inch thick and trimmed of all fat and connective tissue. In general, these tender cuts should be cooked over high heat for a very short time. Most often, they are best when sautéed or grilled over high heat for one to two minutes on each side.

Stew meat is taken from the sections of the animal that do the most work: the neck, shoulder and lower legs. Meat from the bottom round and eye of round also makes good stew meat. Because stew meat is tougher, it must be cooked at a low temperature with moist heat for a long period of time.

Stir-fry strips and cutlets of venison can come from the top round, sirloin butt and loin sections. They should be cut to quarter-inch thickness. Strips should be cooked over high heat for about 30 seconds. Cooking time for cutlets will vary depending upon whether they are breaded and fried or simply sautéed, but generally these thin cuts are cooked no longer than one minute per side.

Ground venison is most often processed from the forequarters, shoulder, neck, flank and shanks. I prefer to have no fat added to our ground venison, especially when it is made from moose, caribou or elk; however, we sometimes add 5% pork fat if the animal was taken from poor habitat, if field-dressing was delayed, or if the meat was in transport for a long time. Since most recipes for cooking ground venison provide plenty of flavor and added moisture, there is no need to add fat. However, for recipes like grilled hamburgers, a little added fat helps make the meat juicy. Ground venison for chili, casseroles and the like should be browned over medium heat, to let it cook gently.

Each recipe includes the number of servings you can expect. I generally allow between 4 and 8 ounces of venison per person. It's often helpful to get a quick glimpse at the amount of time required to prepare a certain recipe, so I've also included prep and assembly time, marinating time where applicable, and cooking time. I hope you'll find this helpful.

Source: U.S. Department of Agriculture

Dishes from Kate's Kitchen

starters

 One year, after taking a seven-point buck on opening morning, I developed a bad case of cabin fever. So a few days later, I decided to fill my doe tag. I took a yearling. When I butchered it, I ended up with only a small amount of meat. Since my husband, Peter, and I were having a post-Thanksgiving dinner party the next evening, I decided to use the meat to create some interesting appetizers.

The next day was spent making a delicious venison tartare (with minced onions, chives and fresh garlic), venison on crackers (paper-thin slices of seared venison, topped with a shaving of gruyère cheese and sliver of white onion), and fondue chunks to be served with several sauces and dips. Lastly, I created venison finger rolls: small venison medallions dipped in Parmesan bread crumbs, sautéed, and wrapped around scallions. Our guests raved about the tenderness and flavor of the meat. Even people who normally don't eat venison enjoyed it. That evening I learned that using venison for finger foods or more formal "starters" can be fun and delicious, particularly when the meat is from a young deer.

Venison Carpaccio with Mustard Sauce

Serves: 4 ✻ Prep Time: 25 minutes

- ½ cup olive oil
- 2 cloves garlic, halved
- ½ lb. venison eye of round, well trimmed
- ¼ cup Dijon mustard
- 2 tablespoons mayonnaise
- 3 tablespoons Horseradish Cream Sauce (page 82)
- 1 tablespoon drained and rinsed capers
- Freshly ground pepper

Combine oil and garlic halves in small glass bowl. Let sit while preparing the venison.

To ensure top flavor, remove all fat, tallow and connective tissue from the venison. Place meat in small baking pan and place in the freezer to firm up. Do not freeze the meat through; it should feel "crunchy" but still yielding when pierced with a knife.

When venison is firm, slice paper-thin with electric meat slicer.* It is very important to slice the venison as thin as possible. Fan the slices on a cold platter.

Remove garlic halves from oil. Whisk mustard into oil until completely combined. Add mayonnaise and whisk until smooth. Drizzle the mustard sauce over the venison. Alternate patterns with the horseradish sauce. Garnish with capers and freshly ground black pepper.

An electric meat slicer is similar to the ones used in delis, in which the meat is fed into a spinning blade. Look for one labeled "for home use."

Note: Carpaccio slices may also be cut into strips and wrapped around breadsticks, as shown in photo. Serve sauces on the side.

Tex-Mex Egg Rolls

Serves: 8 (2 egg rolls each) ✻ Prep Time: 10 minutes ✻ Cooking Time: 25 minutes

- 1 lb. ground venison
- 1 medium onion, finely chopped
- 2 cloves garlic, minced
- ½ cup medium salsa (preferably a smoother type such as Pace Picante)
- ½ teaspoon chili powder
- ¼ teaspoon cumin
- Salt and pepper
- ⅔ cup shredded cheddar cheese
- 1 package egg-roll wraps
- Vegetable oil
- Sour cream and guacamole for serving, optional

In large skillet, cook venison, onion and garlic over medium heat until venison is no longer pink and onion has softened, stirring occasionally to break up meat. Drain grease. Add salsa, chili powder, cumin, and salt and pepper to taste. Simmer for about 5 minutes. Add cheese and stir until mixed thoroughly. Lay 1 egg-roll wrap on work surface; cover remaining wraps with plastic to keep them from drying out. Place a large spoonful of venison mixture on center of wrap and roll as directed on package. Place filled egg roll on platter and repeat with remaining ingredients.

Heat 2 inches oil to 375°F in deep fryer or large pot. Fry egg rolls, two at a time, until golden brown, about 2 minutes. Drain on paper towel–lined plate. Serve with sour cream and guacamole.

Kate's Cooking Tips

Each fondue set contains a pot for the sauce or oil, a stand in which the pot sits, and a burner underneath the stand. For deep-fried fondues, an enameled cast-iron or metal pot is best. If you use this set for dessert or cheese fondues, remember to keep the heat low. Pottery fondue dishes are suitable for cheese fondues but cannot withstand the high heat needed for deep-frying. For dessert fondues, a small fondue pot with a candle burner is adequate to keep the sauce warm.

Keep an eye on the oil when serving the Far East Venison Fondue. Each time meat is added to the pot, the temperature of the oil is reduced and a little oil is lost. If there are many fondue participants, let the oil temperature rise again in between batches, and replenish if necessary with additional hot oil.

FAR EAST VENISON FONDUE

Serves: 4 to 8, depending on other dishes served ✳ Prep Time: 10 minutes
Marinating Time: 1 hour ✳ Cooking Time: 1 to 2 minutes per chunk

A fondue party is an ideal way to entertain guests and, as host, a way to enjoy the party, too. I remember how popular fondue was at parties when I was growing up in the late '60s and early '70s. Each guest had his or her own long, color-coded fork—and if you lost your bread in the cheese, it meant you had to give your partner a kiss. As gawky, eager-eyed teenagers, my sister and I waited with bated breath for the next person to lose a chunk of bread—just to see another one of our neighbors kiss!

Although fondues are not as common nowadays, I still include them in family gatherings. Here's a recipe using chunks of tender venison loin. An Oriental salad makes a nice accompaniment to this fondue.

- 2 lbs. venison loin, well trimmed
- 1/3 cup low-sodium soy sauce
- 1/3 cup dry sherry
- 2 teaspoons brown sugar
- 1 teaspoon ground ginger
- 3 cloves garlic, crushed
- Sauces for dipping: Mustard Sauce, Horseradish Cream Sauce, Garlic Sauce and/or Spicy Far East Dipping Sauce (pages 82-83)
- Vegetable oil

Pat venison dry and cut into 3/4-inch cubes. In large bowl, stir together soy sauce, sherry, brown sugar, ginger and garlic. Add meat and toss to coat. Cover bowl and refrigerate for about 1 hour.

When almost ready to serve, remove venison from marinade, discarding marinade. Pat venison dry and arrange in serving bowl; set aside. Place dipping sauces in amply sized serving bowls, with a serving spoon in each; set aside. Pour enough oil into the fondue pot to fill it one-third full. Transfer oil to a saucepan and heat to 375°F on stove over medium-high heat, checking temperature with deep-frying thermometer. Carefully pour hot oil into fondue pot; keep oil hot over fondue burner. Place bowls of venison and sauces next to fondue pot, along with color-coded fondue forks and small serving plates. Let each person skewer a venison chunk, cook it in oil to desired doneness, and dollop some sauce onto a serving plate for dipping.

Sweet Cherry Peppers with Venison Stuffing

*Serves: 6 * Prep Time: 30 minutes*

- 24 pickled sweet cherry peppers (sold in jars near the pickles)
- ¼ cup olive oil (approx.), divided
- ¼ lb. ground venison
- Salt and pepper
- ½ cup Italian-seasoned bread crumbs
- 2 to 3 tablespoons grated Parmesan cheese
- ¼ teaspoon dehydrated parsley flakes
- 3 cloves garlic, minced

Remove peppers from jar and reserve 1 teaspoon of the liquid. Clean peppers by removing stems and tops, and scooping out core and seeds. Place cleaned peppers on baking sheet; set aside.

In medium skillet, heat 1 teaspoon of the oil over medium heat. Add venison and cook until no longer pink, stirring to break up. Drain grease; season venison with salt and pepper to taste and set aside to cool.

Place cooled venison in food processor and pulse until meat is finely chopped but not mushy. Transfer venison to medium bowl. Add bread crumbs, Parmesan cheese, parsley, garlic and reserved teaspoon of pepper liquid, stirring to mix. Drizzle as much of the remaining oil into the mixture as needed, until mixture is moist and just barely holds together. Stuff peppers with venison mixture, place on a decorative platter and serve.

SVENSKA VENISON MEATBALL PICKS

Serves: 8 ✳ Prep Time: 20 minutes ✳ Cooking Time: 20 minutes

During my seventeenth year, I lived in a small town outside of Stockholm, Sweden. It was there that I experienced my first taste of reindeer. In addition to introducing me to pickled herring, gravlax (pickled salmon), lutefisk and steamed crawfish, my host mother, Iris, used to cook up a wickedly delicious dish of reindeer stroganoff. (Wild game is readily found in most Swedish supermarkets.) I can still recall the savory aroma! Here's a dish that I adapted from her recipe that has become a favorite in our household.

Meatballs:
- 1 lb. ground venison
- 1 egg, beaten
- 3 tablespoons minced onion
- 2 tablespoons cracker crumbs
- ½ teaspoon ginger
- ½ teaspoon garlic powder
- ¼ teaspoon salt
- ¼ teaspoon pepper

Sauce:
- 3 tablespoons unsalted butter
- 3 tablespoons flour
- 1 cup heavy cream
- 1 cup beef broth
- ½ teaspoon paprika
- ¼ teaspoon salt
- ¼ teaspoon white pepper

Heat oven to 325°F. In large bowl, combine all meatball ingredients and mix gently but thoroughly. Measure out the venison mixture by the tablespoon, and shape into tiny meatballs. Place on large sheet pan and bake for about 20 minutes.

While meatballs are cooking, make the sauce: In small saucepan, melt butter over medium-low heat. Stir in flour and cook for about 3 minutes longer, stirring constantly; do not let the mixture turn tan or brown or your sauce will be too dark. Add remaining ingredients and continue stirring until completely smooth. Cook over medium-low heat for about 10 minutes or until desired consistency, stirring frequently.

To serve, place meatballs in chafing dish. Pour sauce over meatballs and serve immediately with toothpicks.

SOUTH-OF-THE-BORDER VENISON DIP

Serves: 8 to 10 ✳ Prep Time: 15 minutes ✳ Assembly Time: 10 minutes or less

- ½ lb. ground venison
- 5 tablespoons water
- 3 tablespoons taco seasoning, divided
- 1 can (16 oz.) refried beans
- 1½ cups sour cream
- 1 cup sliced lettuce (cut into long strips before measuring)
- 1 cup shredded cheddar cheese
- 1 small onion, diced
- Half of a medium green bell pepper, diced
- 2 medium tomatoes, diced
- ¼ cup sliced olives
- Tortilla chips for dipping

Cook venison in medium skillet over medium-high heat until no longer pink, stirring to break up; drain.

Stir in water and half of the taco seasoning. Simmer for about 5 minutes, stirring occasionally. Remove from heat and set aside to cool.

On large round platter, spread refried beans (if they are too stiff to spread, heat for 30 seconds in microwave). Mix remaining taco seasoning into the sour cream. Spread sour cream mixture on top of the cooled refried beans. Spread lettuce evenly over sour cream. Top with cooled venison mixture. Top in layers with the cheese, onion, pepper and tomatoes. Garnish with sliced olives. Serve with tortilla chips.

Use dried spices and herbs carefully. Remember that they have shelf lives of only six months or so; beyond that point, they begin to lose their flavor. If you are not sure of the flavor of a spice, add less than recommended at first. It's always easy to add more, but impossible to remove what's already added.

• • • • • • • • • •

Can you substitute one oil for another? Yes. If you begin a recipe and find the only oil in the house is not what is listed, most often you can substitute with whatever oil you have–or even butter. I note different oils in recipes based upon whether or not I want the flavor of that oil to come through. When I sear or brown meat and don't want any extra flavor, I use canola oil. I specify olive oil if I want that particular flavor as part of the dish. Sometimes I recommend a blend of oil and butter. Butter imparts a unique and delicious flavor to venison, but it burns easily. A combination of oil and butter allows you to cook at a higher heat, without burning, than is possible with butter alone.

VENISON PULGOGI

*Serves: 8 as an appetizer, or 4 as a main dish * Prep Time: 10 minutes*
*Marinating Time: 1 hour * Cooking Time: 10 minutes*

Pulgogi (or bulgogi) is a Korean dish that is usually made with beef. Venison is even better, as you'll discover in this tasty recipe! This also makes a great main dish; serve with white rice, a cucumber salad and some ice-cold Kirin beer.

Marinade:

* 4 scallions, coarsely chopped
* 3 large cloves garlic, finely chopped
* 3 tablespoons soy sauce
* 2 tablespoons sugar
* 2 tablespoons cold water
* 1 tablespoon sesame oil
* 1 tablespoon crushed, toasted sesame seeds
* 2 teaspoons cooking sake or dry white wine
* Freshly ground pepper to taste

* 1¼ lbs. venison tenderloin, slightly frozen
* 1 tablespoon vegetable oil (approx.)
* 1 can (8 oz.) sliced water chestnuts, drained (for appetizers only)

In nonreactive container such as a 2-cup glass measure, combine all marinade ingredients; stir well. Slice venison ¼ inch thick across the grain. Place in shallow dish. Pour marinade over venison, turning gently to coat. Cover and refrigerate for 1 hour.

Prepare grill for high heat; light coals or preheat gas grill. Lightly oil grill rack. Cook venison in batches in a single layer until seared on the outside but still rare, not more than 1 minute per side. If serving as an appetizer, slice cooked medallions in half and place a slice of water chestnut on top. Secure with a toothpick.

Note: A ridged cast-iron steak skillet works well if you don't have a grill available.

VENISON CHILI DIP

*Serves: 6 to 8 * Prep Time: 10 minutes * Cooking Time: 20 minutes*

Serve this tasty warm dip with tortilla chips, corn chips or inch-wide strips of green and red bell peppers.

* 3 slices uncooked bacon, minced
* ½ lb. ground venison
* 2 medium onions, minced
* 2 small poblano chili peppers, minced
* 2 cups canned tomatoes with some liquid, chopped
* 1 cup shredded cheddar cheese
* 2 cloves garlic, minced
* 1 teaspoon sugar
* 1 teaspoon lemon juice
* ½ teaspoon cumin
* ½ teaspoon salt
* ⅛ teaspoon Tabasco sauce

In large skillet, cook bacon over medium heat until it is just beginning to crisp. Add venison and cook until meat is no longer pink, stirring to break up. Add onions and continue cooking until soft, stirring occasionally. Add peppers and tomatoes; reduce heat and let simmer for about 10 minutes. Remove skillet from heat and stir in remaining ingredients.

MUSHROOMS WITH VENISON STUFFING

Serves: 8 ✳ Prep Time: 25 minutes ✳ Cooking Time: 15 minutes

- 1 lb. large mushrooms (about 36)
- 3 teaspoons olive oil, divided
- ¼ lb. ground venison
- 1 teaspoon crumbled dried sage
- 1 teaspoon hot red pepper flakes
- ¼ teaspoon salt
- ⅛ teaspoon white pepper
- ⅓ cup grated onion
- 1 clove garlic, crushed
- ¼ teaspoon dehydrated parsley flakes
- ¼ cup Italian-seasoned bread crumbs
- 1 egg white, lightly beaten
- 1 tablespoon butter, melted

Heat oven to 350°F. Rinse mushrooms and carefully remove stems. Dice about half of the stems and set aside; discard remaining stems. Arrange mushroom caps on rimmed baking sheet; set aside.

In medium skillet, heat 1 teaspoon of the oil over medium heat. Add venison and cook until no longer pink, stirring to break up; as the venison is cooking, add the sage, red pepper, salt and white pepper. Transfer venison mixture to bowl and set aside to cool.

Heat remaining 2 teaspoons oil in same skillet and sauté onion, garlic, parsley and diced mushroom stems until garlic is golden brown. Drain off and discard liquid; set onion mixture aside to cool.

Combine cooled venison and onion mixtures in food processor and process at medium speed for 30 seconds, or until mixture is finely chopped but not mushy. In medium bowl, combine venison mixture with bread crumbs, egg white and butter; mix thoroughly. Transfer to pastry bag and pipe into mushroom caps, or spoon into caps if you don't have a pastry bag. Cover with foil and bake for 15 minutes.

VENISON TERRINE

Serves: 10 * Cooking Time: 3 1/4 hours

Prep Time: 15 minutes after preliminary cooking * Chilling Time: 24 hours

- 3-lb. boneless venison roast
- ¼ teaspoon juniper berries
- ⅛ teaspoon whole coriander seeds
- ¼ teaspoon whole black peppercorns
- 1 bouquet garni*
- 3 large carrots, peeled
- Half of a turnip, peeled
- 2 envelopes (.25 oz. each) unflavored gelatin
- ½ cup cold water
- ⅓ cup chopped fresh parsley
- 3 tablespoons canola oil
- Dash of red wine vinegar
- Salt and pepper

Place venison in Dutch oven and cover with salted water. Add juniper berries, coriander seeds, peppercorns, bouquet garni, whole carrots and turnip. Heat over medium heat to a simmer. Adjust heat as necessary to maintain simmer and cook for approximately 3 hours; check carrots and turnip during cooking and remove when tender.

Remove venison from Dutch oven. Strain cooking broth through cheesecloth-lined colander. Soften gelatin in the ½ cup cold water, then stir it into the hot broth.

Dice venison, carrots and turnip finely and transfer to large bowl. Add parsley, oil, vinegar, and salt and pepper to taste; mix well. Place venison mixture in a terrine dish; there should be about ¼ inch space at the top. Pour broth mixture into the dish, adding enough to cover venison mixture completely. Cover with foil and refrigerate for 24 hours. Turn terrine out onto serving platter. Slice into individual portions and serve with a seasonal salad.

Note: To help free the terrine from the dish, fill the sink with hot water that will come half to three-quarters up the side of the dish. Place the dish in the water for about 30 seconds. Remove from the water and place a plate upside down on top of the terrine dish. Turn both over together and lightly tap the dish to shake the terrine free.

*To make the bouquet garni for this recipe, tie together several sprigs of fresh parsley, a sprig of fresh thyme and a bay leaf.

Tender Venison Finger Rolls

Serves: 6 to 8 ✳ Prep Time: 20 minutes ✳ Marinating Time: 1 hour ✳ Cooking Time: 20 minutes

- 1 bottle (16 oz.) Italian salad dressing
- 1 tablespoon green Tabasco sauce
- 2 lbs. venison loin, cut into ¼-inch-thick slices
- 3 cups all-purpose flour
- ½ teaspoon pepper
- ½ teaspoon garlic powder
- ¼ teaspoon salt
- 2 eggs
- 1 cup milk
- ¼ cup grated Parmesan cheese
- 2 cups seasoned bread crumbs
- 2 cups canola oil (approx.)
- 8 scallions, cut into 1-inch lengths

In nonreactive bowl, mix together dressing and Tabasco; set aside. Place venison slices between 2 pieces of wax paper and flatten to about ⅛-inch thickness with flat side of meat mallet or bottom of saucepan. Add pounded venison to dressing mixture, stirring gently to coat. Cover and refrigerate for about 1 hour.

When venison has marinated for about 1 hour, place flour in large plastic food-storage bag; add pepper, garlic powder and salt. Shake well to mix. In medium bowl, beat together eggs, milk and Parmesan cheese. Place bread crumbs in flat dish.

Remove venison from marinade and pat dry. Flour each medallion, dip into egg mixture, then coat with bread crumbs; transfer to plate in a single layer as each is coated. I like to do this ahead of time and refrigerate to let the breading mixture set, but you may cook them right away if you wish.

In large skillet, heat about ¼ inch of the oil over medium-high heat until hot but not smoking. Fry medallions in small batches for about 1 minute on each side, adding additional oil as necessary. Transfer browned medallions to paper towel–lined plate. When all medallions have been cooked, roll each around a scallion piece and secure with a toothpick. Arrange on platter and serve warm.

San Antonio Venison Cabbage Dip

Serves: 8 to 10 ✳ Prep Time: 10 minutes ✳ Cooking Time: 20 minutes

It was during a whitetail hunting trip to Texas' mesquite country, south of San Antonio, that we were treated to an absolutely delicious appetizer dip like this. The Mexican cook would not reveal her secret ingredients, but I was able to match it pretty closely with the recipe below. When I can find them, I serve blue corn tortilla chips with this warm dip. Enjoy!

- ¾ lb. ground venison
- 1 lb. uncooked bacon, chopped
- 1 head red cabbage, chopped into small bits
- 1 jalapeño pepper, minced (more or less to your taste)
- 1 jar (16 oz.) salsa (preferably a smoother type such as Pace Picante)
- 1 teaspoon chili powder
- Corn tortilla chips for serving

Cook venison in large skillet over medium-high heat until no longer pink, stirring to break up. Drain and set aside. In another large skillet, cook bacon until crispy. Use slotted spoon to transfer bacon to paper towel–lined plate; set aside. Add cabbage and pepper to bacon grease in skillet and cook over medium-high heat until cabbage softens, about 7 minutes. Add salsa and chili powder to skillet, along with cooked bacon and venison. Stir to mix thoroughly, and cook until heated through. Remove from heat and serve warm with tortilla chips.

Starters

19

main meals

Fall is the time of year when hunters are itching to be out of the office and in the woods. For us, the fall is our spring, our renewal. The woods come alive with vivid yellows, reds and oranges, and we savor the crisp, cool morning air as we inhale the unmistakable aroma of the woods that is never more pungent or exceptional than at this time of year.

How many times have you become enveloped by these moments and thought of the frontiersman or pioneer and what he must've felt and sensed during this time of year? Was he daydreaming of which route he'd take to his stand, what technique he would use to either rattle or call in a deer, or what game he might see on an upcoming elk or bison hunt? If you think about it, hunting's natural progression and our thoughts about the pursuit of game haven't changed much. After all, hunting season brings us in tune with Mother Nature as we strain to become one with the woods, fields and earth around us.

In the end, the heart of hunting revolves around its finale: the consumption of the game we take. For thousands of years, venison has served as a main meal for families across the globe. Venison satisfies our yearning for self-sufficiency by allowing us to take pride in our ability to hunt, clean, care for, preserve and cook our own food. It ignites the flames of tradition. Venison is a versatile meat that can be featured in elaborate gatherings, traditional holiday meals or quick dinners for the family. It also adapts well to international cuisines. The recipes that follow offer you a range of these choices, from simple to fancy, using ingredients you'll find right in your kitchen. The recipes are organized by the cuts of meat, starting with roasts, steaks and chops, and ending with ground venison and sausage.

ROAST MUSTARD LOIN OF VENISON

Serves: 8 to 12 ✳ Prep Time: 10 minutes ✳ Marinating Time: 1 to 2 hours ✳ Cooking Time: 30 minutes

- 4- to 5-lb. venison loin, well trimmed (you may also use 2 smaller portions)
- 2 to 3 cups Simple Marinade (page 77)*
- ¼ cup plus 1 tablespoon olive oil, divided
- 1 cup Dijon mustard
- ⅓ cup chopped scallions
- ⅓ cup dry white wine
- ¼ cup bread crumbs
- 4 large cloves garlic, minced
- 1 teaspoon sea salt
- ½ teaspoon crumbled dried sage
- ½ teaspoon crumbled dried thyme
- ¼ teaspoon pepper

Measure venison loin against a large skillet, and cut into halves if necessary to fit skillet. Place venison in nonaluminum pan or bowl; pour marinade over and turn to coat. Cover and refrigerate for 1 to 2 hours, turning occasionally. Remove venison from marinade and pat dry; discard marinade.

Heat oven to 375°F. In large skillet, heat 1 tablespoon of the oil over high heat until it is hot but not smoking. Add venison and quickly sear on all sides. Transfer venison to roasting pan; set aside.

In blender or food processor, combine remaining ¼ cup oil with the mustard, scallions, wine, bread crumbs, garlic, salt, sage, thyme and pepper. Process until smooth; the coating should be thick. Spread coating evenly over venison. Roast to desired doneness (see chart, p. 24), 15 to 17 minutes for medium-rare. Remove venison from oven when internal temperature is 5° less than desired. Tent meat with foil and let rest for 10 to 15 minutes before slicing.

*I sometimes like to use Myron's 20-Gauge Venison Marinade instead of the Simple Marinade. It is a very versatile, all-natural cooking sauce whose ingredients include soy sauce, garlic, red wine, rice wine vinegar, olive oil and spices. It has a rich, slightly malty flavor base, a pungent and peppery bite and subtle juniper flavor points, and works well for a variety of game and fish.

Spit-Roasted Leg of Venison

Serves: 25 to 30 ✳ Prep Time: 10 minutes ✳ Marinating Time: 24 hours ✳ Cooking Time: 2 to 3 hours

Here's a recipe for a deer camp full of hungry hunters. We enjoyed this at the Turtle Creek Camp in the Adirondack Mountains many years ago. While it was cooking, the aroma permeated the woods outside the lodge, where the younger hunters were prompted by the cook to maintain a vigilant watch over the fire!

Marinade:

- 4 to 5 gallons white wine (enough to cover the venison)
- 4 carrots, sliced
- 3 onions, sliced
- 2 heads of garlic, peeled and sliced
- 1 tablespoon dried juniper berries
- 1 tablespoon whole black peppercorns

- 1 whole leg of venison (18 to 20 lbs.), trimmed of as much fat as possible
- Salt and pepper
- 1 lb. butter, melted
- Hunter's Sauce (page 82) for serving, optional

In a nonaluminum container large enough to hold the venison leg, combine 4 gallons of the wine with remaining marinade ingredients. Add leg of venison, and pour in additional wine as needed to cover leg. Refrigerate for 24 hours, turning several times.

When you're ready to cook, prepare a hot wood fire. Remove leg from marinade and pat dry. Secure leg to a spit and season generously with salt and pepper. Strain marinade into large saucepan and heat to boiling; keep warm during cooking to prevent bacterial growth. Place spit over fire and cook for 2 to 3 hours, or until desired doneness, basting often with the melted butter and reserved marinade. The venison should remain slightly rare. Serve with Hunter's Sauce.

Christmas Venison Roast with Baby Mushrooms

Serves: 8 to 10 ✳ Prep Time: 40 minutes ✳ Cooking Time: 1¹/₄ to 1¹/₂ hours

- ³/₄ cup unsalted butter (1¹/₂ sticks), divided
- ¹/₂ cup minced shallots, divided
- ³/₄ lb. fresh spinach leaves
- ¹/₄ lb. fresh baby portobello mushrooms, washed
- ¹/₂ lb. grated Swiss cheese
- 5 slices bacon, cooked and crumbled

- Salt and pepper
- 4-lb. boneless venison roast*
- 1 lemon
- 4 cups brown sauce
- 1¹/₂ cups red wine

First, prepare the stuffing. In large saucepan, melt 6 tablespoons of the butter over medium heat. Add ¹/₄ cup of the shallots. Sauté until translucent. Add spinach and mushrooms; cook about 3 minutes longer. Mix in grated cheese and crumbled bacon. Cook, stirring constantly, until cheese melts and mixture is well blended. Season to taste with salt and pepper. Transfer to medium bowl and place in refrigerator to cool.

Heat oven to 350°F. Butterfly roast, trying to achieve uniform thickness throughout. Season with salt and pepper; squeeze lemon juice liberally over inside of roast, picking off any lemon pips. Spread cooled stuffing evenly over roast. Roll up roast jelly-roll style, rolling with the grain of the meat. Tie roast at 1-inch intervals, using kitchen string.

Melt 4 tablespoons of the remaining butter in large stockpot over medium-high heat. (While a large skillet will also work, the sides of this larger pot will prevent grease from splattering on your stovetop.) Add roast and sear on all sides. Transfer to roasting pan. Roast to desired doneness (see chart, p. 24), 15 to 20 minutes per pound. Remove roast from oven when internal temperature is 5°F less than desired; I prefer rare, so I remove it when the temperature is 125°F. Transfer roast to serving dish and tent loosely with aluminum foil; let rest while you prepare sauce.

In medium saucepan over medium heat, melt remaining 2 tablespoons of butter. Add remaining ¹/₄ cup shallots and sauté for about 2 minutes. Blend in brown sauce and red wine. Reduce heat and simmer, stirring frequently, for about 15 minutes. Check seasoning and adjust as necessary. Pass through fine strainer (or china cap) and serve with roast.

*Since you will be butterflying the roast, you need to start with a boneless roast that is in one piece (not a tied-together roast). Rump or round roasts work well in this recipe.

ADIRONDACK SPINACH VENISON ROAST

Serves: 8 to 10 ❋ Prep Time: 25 minutes ❋ Cooking Time: 1 1/4 to 1 1/2 hours

- ⬩ ½ cup unsalted butter (1 stick), room temperature, divided
- ⬩ 4 cloves garlic, minced, divided
- ⬩ 10 oz. fresh spinach leaves
- ⬩ ½ lb. shredded Gruyère cheese
- ⬩ Salt and pepper
- ⬩ 4-lb. boneless venison roast*

- ⬩ 2 tablespoons lemon juice
- ⬩ 3 slices dry white bread, torn into small pieces
- ⬩ 2 bay leaves, crumbled
- ⬩ 1 teaspoon ground sage
- ⬩ 2 slices uncooked bacon, chopped
- ⬩ Half of a medium onion, chopped

In large skillet, melt 2 tablespoons of the butter over medium heat. Add half of the minced garlic and sauté until golden. Add spinach and sauté until wilted. Add cheese, and salt and pepper to taste. Cook for about 2 minutes longer, stirring constantly. Remove from heat and let cool to room temperature.

Heat oven to 350°F. While the spinach mixture is cooling, butterfly the roast, trying to achieve uniform thickness throughout. Season with salt, pepper and lemon juice. Spread cooled stuffing evenly over meat, keeping an inch away from edges. Roll up roast jelly-roll style, rolling with the grain of the meat. Tie roast at 1-inch intervals, using kitchen string. Place roast on rack in roasting pan. Sprinkle with salt and pepper, and rub remaining 6 tablespoons butter over entire roast.

In food processor or blender, combine bread, bay leaves, sage, bacon, onion and remaining garlic. Pulse on and off, or blend at medium speed, until all ingredients are mixed thoroughly, 30 to 60 seconds. Pat bread-crumb mixture firmly over top and sides of roast.

Roast to desired doneness (see chart, p. 24), 15 to 20 minutes per pound. Remove roast from oven when internal temperature is 5°F less than desired; I prefer rare, so I remove it when the temperature is 125°F. Let roast rest for 10 to 15 minutes before slicing.

*Since you will be butterflying the roast, you need to start with a boneless roast that is in one piece (not a tied-together roast). Rump or round roasts work well in this recipe.

Clarified butter is regular butter from which the milk solids have been removed. Unlike regular butter, it won't burn even at high temperatures, so it is ideal for searing the venison in this recipe. To make clarified butter, melt a stick (or more) in the microwave, or in a small saucepan over low heat. Skim off and discard any foam from the top. Pour the clear yellow liquid into a bowl, leaving the milky residue behind. Cool to room temperature, then chill until hard. If there is any trace of milky residue in the chilled butter, re-melt and pour the clear yellow liquid through cheesecloth.

. . . .

Here's a handy chart for internal temperatures of meat at various stages of doneness:

Amount of Doneness	Internal Temperature
RARE	130° TO 135°
MEDIUM-RARE	135° TO 140°
MEDIUM	140° TO 145°
MEDIUM-WELL	145° TO 155°
WELL DONE	155° TO 160°

VENISON FILET WELLINGTON

Serves: 5 to 8 ✳ Prep Time: 45 minutes ✳ Cooking Time: 10 to 15 minutes

Here's an elegant dish that will knock the socks off your deer-camp buddies. It may look complex, but it really is quite simple. From start to finish, Venison Filet Wellington will take about an hour. Read the directions at least once before preparing this dish, and you will see how quickly it comes together. Have all your ingredients ready, to make the assembly smooth and quick. Don't miss trying this recipe; it is well worth the effort.

- 2- to 3-lb. venison loin, well trimmed
- 2 tablespoons clarified butter, room temperature
- 2 to 4 slices bacon
- 2 tablespoons butter
- 3 tablespoons olive oil
- 2 tablespoons chopped shallots
- ½ lb. fresh white or straw mushrooms, finely chopped
- 1 egg, separated
- 2 tablespoons cold water
- 1 sheet (half of a 17¼-oz. pkg.) frozen puff pastry, thawed per package directions
- Flour for rolling out pastry
- 1 cup shredded fresh spinach leaves
- ½ cup shredded Swiss cheese
- Hunter's Sauce (page 82)

Heat oven to 325°F. Heat a large, heavy-bottomed skillet over medium-high heat. While skillet is heating, rub venison with clarified butter. Add loin to hot skillet and sear to a deep brown color on all sides. Transfer loin to dish and set aside to cool to room temperature. Meanwhile, add bacon to same skillet and fry until cooked but not crisp. Set aside on paper towel–lined plate.

While the loin is cooling, prepare the filling. In medium skillet, melt the 2 tablespoons butter in the oil over medium heat. Add shallots and sauté until golden, stirring constantly; don't let the shallots brown or they will become bitter. Add mushrooms and sauté until most of the liquid evaporates. Set mushroom mixture aside to cool.

Beat egg white lightly in small bowl. In another small bowl, lightly beat egg yolk and water. Set both bowls aside.

To prepare the shell, roll out pastry on lightly floured surface to a rectangle 1 to 2 inches larger on all sides than the loin. Spread cooled mushroom mixture over the pastry, leaving 1 inch clear around the edges. Layer the spinach, cheese and bacon in a thin strip over the center; the strip should be about as wide as the loin. Place loin on top of bacon. Brush edges of pastry with egg white; this will help hold the pastry shell together while it is baking. Wrap pastry around loin and crimp edges very well to seal. Turn pastry-wrapped loin over so the seam side is down. Place onto baking sheet. Brush pastry with egg yolk mixture; this will provide a beautiful glaze to the Wellington.

Bake for 10 to 15 minutes, or until pastry is golden brown. The loin should have reached an internal temperature of 130°F. Remove from oven. Slice into individual portions and serve immediately with Hunter's Sauce.

When roasting venison, make sure that the roasting pan is slightly larger than the roast, but not too much larger. If the pan is too large, the drippings will spread out and burn.

• • • • • • • • •

Make sure that large cuts of venison are at room temperature before cooking. This way they will cook more uniformly.

• • • • • • • • •

When time allows, after cutlets are breaded, place them in the refrigerator for 2 to 3 minutes. I like to do this to "set" the breading before frying.

VENISON TENDERLOIN SICILIANO

*Serves: 4 * Prep Time: 10 minutes * Cooking Time: 10 minutes or less*

Peter and I were hunting Rocky Mountain elk in northern New Mexico and stopped one evening in the beautiful town of Taos for dinner. We dined on a version of this dish, and were fortunate enough to have the chef share the recipe with us. Although I have altered it over the years, this recipe is simple yet offers a deliciously rich flavor. Marsala, a sweet, fortified wine from Sicily, can be found in your local liquor store.

- 1 cup flour
- Salt and pepper
- 1 lb. venison tenderloin, cut into ½-inch-thick medallions
- 2 tablespoons butter
- 2 tablespoons canola oil
- 1½ cups mushrooms, sliced
- 3 tablespoons minced shallots
- ½ cup Marsala wine
- 1½ cups brown sauce or beef gravy
- 1 tablespoon chopped fresh parsley

Place flour in large plastic food-storage bag; add salt and pepper to taste and shake well to mix. Add medallions, 2 at a time, and shake to coat. Transfer medallions to a plate as they are coated.

In large skillet, melt butter in oil over medium-high heat. Add medallions and cook until browned on first side. Turn medallions; add mushrooms and shallots. Cook for about 2 minutes longer. Add Marsala and heat to simmering. Add brown sauce and parsley and heat to simmering again. Simmer for 2 minutes longer. Serve immediately.

CHICKEN-FRIED VENISON

*Serves: 6 * Prep Time: 10 minutes * Marinating Time: 2 hours*
Cooking Time: 15 minutes

Serve this classic southern-style dish with a brown sauce and garlic mashed potatoes.

- 2 lbs. venison loin, cut into ½-inch-thick medallions
- 2 cups milk
- 4 cloves garlic, minced
- 1 tablespoon cayenne pepper, divided
- 1½ teaspoons black pepper
- ½ teaspoon onion salt
- 1 egg
- ¼ teaspoon salt
- 1 cup all-purpose flour
- ¼ cup canola oil (approx.), divided

With flat side of a meat mallet or the bottom of a saucepan, pound medallions to flatten slightly. In bowl, combine milk, garlic, 1½ teaspoons of the cayenne, the black pepper and onion salt. Add medallions; cover and refrigerate for 2 hours.

When ready to cook, transfer medallions to a plate and set aside. Add egg to milk mixture and beat together. Return medallions to milk mixture. In large bowl, mix remaining 1½ teaspoons cayenne and the salt with the flour. Dredge medallions in flour.

In cast-iron skillet, heat 1 tablespoon of the canola oil over medium-high heat until hot but not smoking. Place 1 or 2 medallions at a time into skillet and cook for 2 to 3 minutes per side, until golden brown. Transfer to heated platter and repeat with remaining medallions, adding additional oil as necessary.

Blackened Cajun Medallions of Venison

Serves: 4 * Prep Time: 10 minutes * Cooking Time: 10 minutes or less

Open the windows or turn on a powerful vent fan when you're cooking this, as it will produce a lot of smoke! This dish is excellent served with the Wild Rice Casserole on page 88.

Blackened Seasoning Mix
- 2 teaspoons paprika
- 2 teaspoons crumbled dried thyme
- 1 teaspoon black pepper
- 1 teaspoon garlic powder
- 1 teaspoon cumin
- 1 teaspoon crumbled dried oregano
- 1 teaspoon sugar
- ½ teaspoon cayenne pepper
- ½ teaspoon salt

- 4 venison loin medallions (4 to 6 oz. each), ¾ to 1 inch thick
- 2 tablespoons unsalted butter, melted
- 1 tablespoon butter

In small bowl, stir together all seasoning-mix ingredients. Pat medallions dry. Brush each side with melted butter. Sprinkle generously on both sides with seasoning mix, and pat to help seasonings adhere.

Heat large cast-iron skillet over high heat. When hot, add the tablespoon of butter. When butter just stops foaming, add medallions and cook for 2 to 3 minutes on each side, depending upon the thickness of the steaks. Serve immediately.

Applejack Venison Medallions

Serves: 6 * Prep Time: 10 minutes * Cooking Time: 20 minutes

I like to serve this with au gratin potatoes, and a dish of green peas garnished with pearl onions.

- 6 venison loin medallions (4 oz. each), ¾ inch thick
- Salt
- ½ cup clarified butter (see sidebar on page 24), divided
- 3 tablespoons applejack brandy, preferably Calvados
- 1 large shallot, minced
- 1 teaspoon crushed black and red peppercorn blend
- ½ teaspoon cornstarch
- 2 cups beef broth (prepared from beef bouillon granules)
- 1 cup heavy cream, room temperature

Pat medallions dry and sprinkle both sides with salt to taste. In large skillet, melt ¼ cup of the clarified butter over medium-high heat. Add medallions in a single layer and sear on both sides. Transfer medallions to a plate; pour excess butter from the skillet and lower heat to medium. Return medallions to skillet and add brandy. Cook until brandy is warm. Remove skillet from heat and carefully ignite brandy with long-handled match. When flames die out, transfer medallions to plate; set aside and keep warm.

Melt remaining ¼ cup butter in same skillet over medium heat. Add shallot and peppercorns, and sauté until shallot is translucent. Meanwhile, blend cornstarch and broth in measuring cup or small bowl. When shallot is translucent, pour broth mixture into skillet, stirring constantly. Cook until broth is reduced to about half, stirring frequently. Add 2 tablespoons of the reduced sauce to the cream and mix well (leave the cream in its measuring cup, or place in a small bowl); this raises the temperature of the cream to prevent curdling when cream is added to the sauce. Reduce heat under skillet to low and add cream mixture. Simmer until the mixture is reduced to saucelike consistency, stirring frequently. Return medallions to skillet and re-warm them briefly before serving.

VENISON MEDALLIONS WITH HERBED CHEESE SAUCE

Serves: 2 ✳ Prep Time: 5 minutes ✳ Cooking Time: 15 minutes

Serve these tasty medallions with twice-baked potatoes and steamed broccoli.

- 1½ cups all-purpose flour
- Salt and black pepper
- ½ cup Boursin herb cheese, or any soft herbed cheese
- ¾ cup heavy cream
- 2 tablespoons olive oil
- 6 venison loin medallions (3 oz. each), ½ inch thick
- ½ cup white wine
- Cayenne pepper

Place flour in large plastic food-storage bag; add salt and black pepper to taste and shake well to mix. Set aside. In small bowl, blend herbed cheese and heavy cream with whisk or slotted spoon; set aside.

Heat oil in heavy-bottom skillet over medium-high heat. Dredge medallions in seasoned flour. Add to skillet and sear well on both sides. Transfer medallions to warm plate; set aside and keep warm. Add wine to skillet and cook for about a minute, stirring to loosen any browned bits. Add cream mixture. Stir well to blend, and season with salt, pepper and cayenne to taste. Cook over medium heat, stirring frequently, until sauce thickens slightly; do not boil. Pour sauce over medallions and serve.

Canadian Barren-Ground Caribou Tenderloin

Serves: 2 ❋ Prep Time: 10 minutes ❋ Cooking Time: 10 to 15 minutes

- 3 tablespoons canola oil, divided
- 3 medium yellow onions, thinly sliced
- 4 caribou or venison tenderloins
  (3 oz. each), well trimmed
- 3 tablespoons minced shallots
- 1/2 cup thickly sliced fresh mushrooms
- 1 cup heavy cream, room temperature
- 1/2 cup Madeira wine
- 1/4 cup unsalted butter
- Salt and white pepper

In medium skillet, heat 1 tablespoon of the oil over medium-high heat until it is hot but not smoking. Add onions and sauté until browned. Remove from heat; set aside and keep warm.

While onions are cooking, pound each of the tenderloin pieces with flat side of meat mallet until very thin. In large skillet, heat the remaining 2 tablespoons oil over high heat until it is hot but not smoking. Sauté flattened tenderloins for about 1 minute on each side. Transfer to a warmed platter; set aside and keep warm.

Add shallots to same skillet and cook over medium-high heat, stirring constantly, for about 1 minute. Add mushrooms and sauté until tender. Add cream, wine and butter. Cook until slightly thickened, stirring constantly. Add salt and pepper to taste.

To serve, divide onions between 2 dinner plates. Top each with 2 cutlets. Pour mushroom sauce over the top.

Sweet Moose Loin Roast

Serves: 12 to 14 ❋ Prep Time: 15 minutes ❋ Cooking Time: 1 to 1 1/2 hours

- 1/2 cup light molasses
- 1 tablespoon dark brown sugar
- 1 tablespoon sesame oil
- 4 cloves garlic, minced
- 3 tablespoons canola oil
- 4-lb. moose loin portion, well trimmed
- 1 teaspoon sea salt
- 1 teaspoon freshly ground pepper
- Horseradish Cream Sauce (page 82)

Heat oven to 425°F. In small bowl, combine molasses, brown sugar, sesame oil and garlic. Mix well and set aside.

In large skillet, heat canola oil over high heat until it is hot but not smoking. Add moose loin and quickly sear on all sides; if the loin is too large for the skillet, cut it into halves and sear in 2 batches.

Place seared loin on rack in large roasting pan. Season with salt and pepper on all sides. Spread molasses mixture all over loin. Place in oven and reduce temperature to 350°F. Roast to desired doneness (see chart, p. 24), 13 to 18 minutes per pound. Remove roast from oven when internal temperature is 5° less than desired; I prefer rare, so I remove it when the temperature is 125°F. Let meat rest for 10 to 15 minutes before slicing. Serve with Horseradish Cream Sauce.

Roast Venison with Green Peppercorn Sauce

Serves: 6 to 8 ❋ Prep Time: 5 minutes ❋ Cooking Time: 1 1/4 to 1 1/2 hours

- 1/4 teaspoon salt
- 1/8 teaspoon pepper
- 1/8 teaspoon garlic powder
- 3-lb. venison roast, preferably boneless
- 2 tablespoons butter
- 2 tablespoons olive oil
- 1/3 cup canned or bottled green peppercorns, drained
- 2 cups light cream
- 1 cup beef bouillon

Heat oven to 325°F. Mix the salt, pepper and garlic powder, then rub over entire roast. In Dutch oven, melt butter in oil over medium-high heat. Add roast and brown on all sides. Place in oven and roast, uncovered, to desired doneness (see chart, p. 24), 15 to 20 minutes per pound. Remove roast from oven when internal temperature is 5° less than desired; I prefer rare, so I remove it when the temperature is 125°F. Transfer roast to serving dish and tent loosely with aluminum foil; let rest while you prepare sauce.

Remove excess fat from Dutch oven. Place pan over medium heat on stovetop. Add green peppercorns, slightly crushing some of the grains. Add cream and bouillon. Heat to boiling, then cook until liquid is thickened and smooth. Season to taste with salt and pepper. Slice roast and serve with green peppercorn sauce.

Venison Cutlet Delight

Serves: 4 to 6 * Prep Time: 20 minutes * Cooking Time: 15 minutes

- 1 cup all-purpose flour
- Salt and pepper
- 2 eggs
- 1½ cups milk
- 1 cup Italian-seasoned bread crumbs
- ¼ cup grated Parmesan cheese
- 1 teaspoon garlic powder
- 8 venison cutlets (about 4 oz. each), pounded to ¼-inch thickness
- ½ cup canola oil (approx.)
- 1 can (10 oz.) whole asparagus, drained
- ½ lb. bacon, cooked and crumbled
- ½ lb. Swiss cheese, sliced

Heat oven to 400°F. Place flour in large plastic food-storage bag; add salt and pepper to taste and shake well to mix. In medium bowl, beat together eggs and milk. In large bowl, mix together bread crumbs, Parmesan cheese and garlic powder.

Pat cutlets dry. Flour each cutlet, dip into egg mixture, then coat with bread crumb mixture; transfer to plate in a single layer as each is coated.

In large skillet, heat about ¼ inch of the oil over medium heat until hot but not smoking. Fry cutlets in small batches until just browned on both sides, adding additional oil as necessary. Transfer browned cutlets to paper towel–lined plate.

When all cutlets have been browned, arrange in single layer on large baking sheet. Place 2 asparagus spears on each cutlet. Top each with a little crumbled bacon, then place a slice of Swiss cheese over each. Place in oven just until cheese melts, 1 to 2 minutes. Serve immediately.

Steak with Caper-Mustard Sauce

Serves: 4 * Prep Time: 10 minutes * Cooking Time: 20 minutes

- 1 cup all-purpose flour
- ½ teaspoon salt
- ½ teaspoon pepper
- 4 boneless venison steaks (about 6 oz. each), well trimmed
- 2 tablespoons canola oil
- 1 medium onion, finely chopped
- 1 shallot, minced
- 2 tablespoons red wine vinegar
- ¼ cup beef broth (prepared from beef bouillon granules)
- ¼ cup nonfat plain yogurt
- 2 tablespoons drained and rinsed capers
- 1 tablespoon Dijon mustard
- 2 tablespoons chopped fresh parsley

Place flour in large plastic food-storage bag; add salt and pepper and shake well to mix. Pat steaks dry, and dredge steaks in seasoned flour.

In heavy-bottomed skillet, heat oil over medium-high heat until hot but not smoking. Add steaks and cook for about 2 minutes on each side for medium-rare, or as desired. Transfer steaks to platter; set aside and keep warm.

Add onion, shallot and vinegar to same skillet. Sauté until vinegar has cooked away. Lower heat to medium and add broth, then yogurt. Simmer until mixture is reduced by half; do not allow mixture to boil.

Remove skillet from heat. Stir in capers and mustard. Blend together thoroughly, then pour over steaks. Sprinkle with parsley and serve.

Curry Grilled Venison Steaks

Serves: 4 * Prep Time: 5 minutes * Cooking Time: 10 minutes or less

- 2 teaspoons salt
- 1 teaspoon coarsely ground pepper
- 1 teaspoon curry powder
- ½ teaspoon garlic powder
- 2 tablespoons red wine vinegar
- 4 boneless venison steaks (about 6 oz. each), ¾ inch thick, well trimmed

Heat broiler, or prepare grill for high heat by lighting coals or preheating gas grill. In small bowl, mix together salt, pepper, curry powder and garlic powder. Add vinegar to glass baking dish. Add steaks, turning to coat both sides. Sprinkle steaks with half of the curry mixture; turn and sprinkle with remaining curry mixture.

If broiling indoors, place steaks on lightly greased rack in broiling pan. With oven rack at closest position to heat, broil steaks for 2 minutes. Turn steaks and continue broiling for 2 or 3 minutes for medium-rare, or until desired doneness.

If grilling outdoors, grill for 2 to 3 minutes on each side for medium-rare, or until desired doneness.

"Too Late" Venison Cutlet Gruyère

Serves: 6 ∗ Prep Time: 10 minutes ∗ Cooking Time: 10 to 15 minutes

One of the fun parts of hunting is naming deer stands. Peter and I have one we call "Torn Shirt" because he tore his shirt while putting it up. Another is named "Four Point" because the first buck shot out of the stand was a four-point. The "Too Late" stand is near a pine-covered ridge, and got its name because once the deer reach the peak of the ridge and come out from the cover to cross to the other side, it's too late. I first prepared the following tasty recipe with a buck taken from this stand.

- ¼ cup all-purpose flour
- Salt and pepper
- 2 eggs
- ½ cup milk
- 3 cups seasoned bread crumbs
- ¼ teaspoon garlic powder
- 12 venison cutlets (about 4 oz. each), pounded as needed to even thickness
- ½ cup olive oil (approx.)
- 1½ cups seasoned tomato sauce
- 2 large beefsteak-type tomatoes, thinly sliced
- 12 slices Gruyère or Swiss cheese

Heat broiler. Place flour in large plastic food-storage bag; add salt and pepper to taste and shake well to mix. In medium bowl, beat together eggs and milk. Combine bread crumbs and garlic powder in wide, flat dish and stir to mix. Blot cutlets with paper towel.

Working with one cutlet at a time, add to bag of flour and shake to coat. Tap off excess flour, then dip floured cutlet into egg mixture. Dredge in bread crumb mixture; set aside on a plate. Repeat with remaining cutlets.

In large skillet, heat about ¼ inch of the oil over medium heat until it is hot but not smoking. Fry cutlets in batches, adding additional oil as necessary, until cutlets are golden brown on both sides and not quite done to taste; transfer cutlets to sheet pan as they are browned.

In small saucepan, heat tomato sauce over low heat; cover and keep warm. Place 1 or 2 tomato slices and 1 cheese slice on top of each cutlet. Place sheet pan under broiler just long enough to melt the cheese.

Ladle about ¼ cup warm tomato sauce on each of 6 plates and place 2 cutlets on top; or, place 2 cutlets on each plate and drizzle tomato sauce around the cutlets. Serve hot.

VENISON STEAK WITH RED CURRANTS

Serves: 4 ✳ Prep Time: 30 minutes ✳ Cooking Time: 10 minutes or less

While hunting red stag at a 5,000-acre ranch owned by the German baron Josef von Kerckerinck, I learned about the European fondness for pairing fruit with wild game—something I'd not encountered very frequently here in the States. Since then, I've created many delicious variations on this theme. If you're fond of such a flavor combination, I'm sure you'll enjoy this recipe as much as I do. If this pairing is new for you, give it a try; it will give your game a delicious new taste. As it turned out, I took a 16-point stag on that hunt; the meat was delicious with this recipe.

* 2 cups red wine
* ½ cup sugar
* 2 pears, peeled, halved and cored
* 4 venison steaks (8 oz. each), well trimmed
* Salt and pepper
* 2 tablespoons butter
* 2 tablespoons canola or corn oil
* 2 shallots, chopped
* ¼ cup red wine vinegar
* 1 cup beef broth
* ¼ cup heavy cream
* ⅓ cup red currants*

In medium saucepan, combine wine and sugar and cook over medium heat, stirring constantly, until sugar dissolves. Increase heat slightly and cook until mixture is steaming but not bubbling. Add pears and cook for about 3 minutes. Remove pan from heat; set aside and keep warm.

Pat steaks with paper towel; season to taste with salt and pepper. In medium skillet, melt butter in oil over medium-high heat. Add steaks and sear on both sides. Cook until medium-rare, about 2 minutes per side. Transfer to dish; set aside and keep warm.

Add shallots to same skillet and sauté over medium-high heat until fragrant; do not burn. Add vinegar, stirring to loosen browned bits, and continue cooking until liquid has cooked almost completely away. Add broth and boil until reduced by about half. Reduce heat to medium, stir in cream and simmer until reduced to saucelike consistency; stir frequently and remove skillet from heat temporarily if sauce begins to boil over. Add salt and pepper to taste. Add red currants to sauce and cook, stirring gently, until heated through. Serve steak with red currant sauce, garnishing each with poached pear half.

Available in most gourmet markets and specialty food stores. Black currants, not as prominent in the food markets, also work well here. Just increase the amount to ½ cup.

STEAK AU POIVRE

Serves: 4 ✳ Prep Time: 10 minutes ✳ Marinating Time: 2 to 6 hours ✳ Cooking Time: 15 minutes

This dish is a favorite of mine; I serve it frequently when we have dinner guests.

- 2 tablespoons coarsely crushed black peppercorns
- 2 tablespoons coarsely crushed white peppercorns
- 1/8 teaspoon hot red pepper flakes
- 8 venison loin medallions (3 oz. each), 1/2 inch thick
- 1 tablespoon canola oil
- 2 tablespoons chopped shallots
- 2 tablespoons brandy
- 1 cup beef broth
- 2 tablespoons Dijon mustard
- 1/8 teaspoon Worcestershire sauce
- 1/2 cup heavy cream, room temperature

In small bowl, mix together the peppercorns and red pepper flakes. Press peppercorn mixture into both sides of the steaks. Place on plate; cover and refrigerate for 2 to 6 hours. Bring steaks to room temperature before cooking.

In large skillet, heat oil over medium-high heat until hot but not smoking. Add medallions and sear on one side. Turn medallions, then add shallots to skillet and cook until steaks are seared on second side. Carefully add brandy. Allow to warm for a moment. Remove from heat and carefully ignite with long-handled match. When flames die out, transfer medallions to platter; set aside and keep warm.

Add broth, mustard and Worcestershire sauce to skillet. Heat to simmering over medium heat; cook for about 1 minute, stirring constantly. Add cream and heat to simmering. If the steaks are warm, serve immediately with the sauce ladled over the top of the steaks. If they have cooled slightly, add the steaks back to the skillet to heat through; serve immediately.

VENISON PARMIGIANA

Serves: 6 ✳ Prep Time: 10 minutes ✳ Cooking Time: 25 minutes

Serve with a side of hot linguini, fresh romaine salad and garlic bread with "the works"!

- 1/4 cup all-purpose flour
- Salt and pepper
- 2 eggs
- 1/2 cup milk
- 3 cups seasoned bread crumbs
- 1/4 teaspoon garlic powder
- 12 venison cutlets (3 to 4 oz. each), pounded as needed to even thickness
- 1/2 cup olive oil (approx.)
- 4 cups tomato sauce
- 1 lb. mozzarella cheese, shredded
- 1 1/2 cups grated Parmesan cheese

Place flour in large plastic food-storage bag; add salt and pepper to taste and shake well to mix. In medium bowl, beat together eggs and milk. In large bowl, mix together bread crumbs and garlic powder.

Pat cutlets dry. Flour each cutlet, dip into egg mixture, then coat with bread crumb mixture; transfer to plate in a single layer as each is coated.

Heat broiler. In large skillet, heat about 1/4 inch of the oil over medium-high heat until hot but not smoking. Fry cutlets in small batches until just browned on both sides, adding additional oil as necessary. Transfer browned cutlets to paper towel–lined plate.

Spread a thick layer of tomato sauce on the bottom of a large rectangular baking dish (the dish needs to be large enough to hold all cutlets in a single layer; use 2 smaller dishes if necessary). Place browned cutlets on sauce in a single layer. Top each cutlet with about 1/4 cup tomato sauce, some mozzarella cheese and 2 tablespoons Parmesan cheese. Place dish under broiler and broil until cheeses melt and bubble. Serve immediately.

WESTERN STYLE BAR-B-QUE
VENISON CHOPS

❦

Serves: 6 ✳ Prep Time: 30 minutes ✳ Marinating Time: 1 to 4 hours
Cooking Time: 10 minutes or less

I was practicing shooting my five arrows for the day, when out of the corner of my eye I thought I saw a deer bolt across our food plot. I slowly put my bow down and glanced across the clearing, resting my gaze momentarily on each apple tree to see if there were any hungry customers munching away. Suddenly, another deer jumped out from the thick cover and darted across. I patiently watched these two young bucks run in and out of the woods, quickly grabbing apples and flicking their tails nervously. As I moved uphill to see what might be spooking them, I spotted a small black bear cub just down the hill. Not knowing where the sow was, I retreated to the safety of my deck, just before the cub bawled out to the sow. Had it been deer season at the time, I probably would not have ever seen the bear cub, as the 5-pointer would not have gotten away from my arrow.

This leads me to a pointer for deer chops. If your chops are from a young deer, they will probably be so tender that they won't need much marinating; in fact, you could probably just sprinkle the trimmed chops with pepper and grill them. In the recipe below, use the shorter marinating time for young chops, just for a flavor boost. If your chops are from a more mature deer, use the longer marinating time, which will help tenderize the meat. Serve with a potato salad and grilled corn on the cob.

Barbecue Sauce:
* 1/2 cup white wine vinegar
* 1/4 lemon, diced
* 1 teaspoon ground coriander seed
* 1/2 teaspoon cumin
* 1/4 teaspoon cayenne pepper
* 1/8 teaspoon paprika
* Hot red pepper flakes and black pepper to taste

* 6 venison chops (6 oz. each), about 1/2 inch thick, well trimmed

To prepare the sauce: Combine all sauce ingredients in small nonaluminum saucepan. Simmer over medium-low heat for about 20 minutes. Let cool.

Place chops in glass pan and cover with cooled sauce. Cover and refrigerate for 1 to 4 hours.

When you're ready to cook, prepare grill for high heat; light coals or preheat gas grill (high heat is necessary to sear the chops while still maintaining medium-rare doneness). Remove chops from marinade. Place on grate and grill for 2 to 4 minutes on each side; the length of time will depend upon the thickness of the chops and desired doneness.

PAN-FRIED VENISON WITH CREAMY
PEPPERCORN SAUCE

Serves: 8 ✳ Prep Time: 10 minutes ✳ Cooking Time: 30 minutes

- ¾ cup white wine vinegar
- ¾ cup sauterne or sweet white wine
- 1 tablespoon whole black peppercorns
- 1 tablespoon dried whole green peppercorns*
- 1 tablespoon dried whole pink peppercorns*
- 2 cups heavy cream, room temperature
- 2 cups all-purpose flour
- 1 teaspoon salt
- 1 teaspoon pepper
- ½ teaspoon garlic powder
- 3 lbs. venison steaks
- 2 tablespoons canola oil

In heavy nonstick saucepan, stir together vinegar, sauterne and peppercorns. Heat to boiling over medium-high heat. Boil until liquid is reduced to about half, about 10 minutes, stirring frequently. Reduce heat to medium, stir in cream and simmer until liquid is reduced to about 1¼ cups; stir frequently and remove pan from heat temporarily if sauce begins to boil over. Keep sauce warm over very low heat.

Place flour in large plastic food-storage bag; add salt, pepper and garlic powder and shake well to mix. Add steaks and toss to coat. In large, heavy skillet, heat oil over medium-high heat until hot but not smoking. Add steaks and cook for about 2 minutes on each side, or until desired doneness. Serve steaks with peppercorn sauce.

Available at specialty foods shops and some supermarkets and also from Specialty World Foods (page 122). The green and pink peppercorns add color and contribute subtle flavors to the sauce; however, you may prepare the sauce using black peppercorns only.

Venison Steak Forrestiere

Serves: 8 ✳ Prep Time: 10 minutes ✳ Cooking Time: 15 minutes

- 1½ cups all-purpose flour
- Salt and pepper
- 8 boneless venison steaks (4 to 6 oz. each), well trimmed
- 2 tablespoons canola oil
- 1 cup sliced mushrooms*
- ½ cup crumbled cooked bacon
- 1 tablespoon minced garlic
- 1 tablespoon chopped fresh parsley
- ½ cup red wine
- ¾ cup brown sauce or beef gravy

Place flour in large plastic food-storage bag; add salt and pepper to taste and shake well to mix. Pat steaks dry, and dredge in seasoned flour.

In large skillet, heat oil over medium-high heat until hot but not smoking. Add steaks, and cook for 2 to 3 minutes on each side. Transfer steaks to plate; set aside and keep warm.

Add mushrooms, bacon, garlic and parsley to skillet; stir well. Add wine, stirring to loosen any browned bits. Add brown sauce and stir well. Return steaks to skillet; simmer for 5 minutes.

To add flavor, try using half baby portobello mushrooms.

Venison Steak Fajitas

Serves: 5 ✳ Prep Time: 20 minutes ✳ Cooking Time: 7 to 8 hours, largely unattended

When the summer days are getting longer, most of us want to spend our time out- doors on a bass pond rather than in the kitchen. This is one of my favorite dishes for times like that. You can start it in the slow cooker at noontime, or a little before, and you'll have a late, quick meal to enjoy while you discuss how "the big one" got away!

- 2 lbs. boneless venison steak
- 2 limes, halved
- 1½ cups tomato juice
- 3 cloves garlic, minced
- 1 tablespoon minced fresh parsley
- 2 teaspoons chili powder
- 1 teaspoon crumbled dried oregano
- 1 teaspoon ground cumin
- ½ teaspoon ground coriander seed
- ½ teaspoon salt
- ¼ teaspoon pepper
- 1 medium onion, sliced
- 1 green bell pepper, sliced
- 1 red bell pepper, sliced
- 1 jalapeño pepper, thinly sliced
- 10 flour tortillas
- Accompaniments: Sour cream, chopped tomatoes, guacamole, salsa or grated cheddar cheese

Slice venison thinly across the grain. Place slices in medium bowl. Squeeze limes over venison slices, picking out any seeds. Toss to coat well. Place venison in slow cooker. Combine tomato juice, garlic, parsley, chili powder, oregano, cumin, coriander, salt and pepper; stir to mix well. Pour over venison. Cover and cook on LOW for 6 to 7 hours.

Add the onion, bell peppers and jalapeño. Re-cover and cook for 1 hour longer. Warm the tortillas in the microwave. With a slotted spoon, put about ½ cup of the venison mixture in each flour tortilla. Add one or more accompaniments as desired; roll up tortilla.

Hunter's Venison Stroganoff

Serves: 4 ✳ Prep Time: 10 minutes ✳ Cooking Time: 30 minutes

When time is short but it's just the right weather for a hearty meal, try this simple version of the classic main course. Serve it over egg noodles, to catch all of the savory sauce.

- 1 to 1¼ lbs. boneless venison sirloin steak, cut into ¾-inch strips
- Salt and pepper
- 2 tablespoons vegetable or canola oil
- 1 lb. button or baby portobello mushrooms, sliced
- 1 large yellow onion, thinly sliced
- 1 tablespoon all-purpose flour
- 1 cup beef broth
- ½ cup dry red wine
- ¾ cup sour cream, room temperature
- 1½ teaspoons paprika

Sprinkle venison strips with salt and pepper to taste. In large nonstick skillet, heat oil over high heat. Add venison strips in batches and cook, stirring frequently, until browned on all sides. Use slotted spoon to transfer browned strips to large bowl after each batch. When all venison has been browned and removed from skillet, add mushrooms and onion to skillet. Sauté until browned, about 12 minutes. Sprinkle flour into skillet, stirring constantly. Add broth and wine. Reduce heat to medium and simmer, stirring frequently, until sauce thickens and coats spoon, about 5 minutes. Reduce heat to low. Return venison and any accumulated juices to skillet. Mix in sour cream and paprika. Cook, stirring frequently, until heated through, about 3 minutes; do not boil or the sour cream may separate. Check for seasoning, and add salt and pepper as necessary.

GRILLED ELK STEAK FLORENTINE

Serves: 4 ✳ Prep Time: 10 minutes ✳ Cooking Time: 15 minutes

- 2 elk steaks (1½ lbs. each), about 1½ inches thick
- 2 tablespoons coarsely crushed black peppercorns
- 1 tablespoon plus 1½ teaspoons crumbled dried sage
- 1 tablespoon crumbled dried thyme
- 1 tablespoon crumbled dried rosemary
- 1½ teaspoons garlic powder
- 2 tablespoons sea salt
- ½ cup olive oil plus additional for brushing steaks
- 8 cloves garlic, thinly sliced
- 3 lbs. fresh spinach leaves
- 2 tablespoons lemon juice
- Salt and pepper
- Grated Parmesan cheese for garnish

Prepare grill for high heat; light coals or preheat gas grill. Trim steaks of all fat and connective tissue. Pat dry. In small bowl, combine crushed peppercorns, sage, thyme, rosemary, garlic powder and sea salt. Press mixture evenly into both sides of steaks. Brush steaks gently with oil. Place on grate directly over hot coals and sear both sides. Cook for 3 to 5 minutes on each side, or until internal temperature is about 125°F (rare). Transfer to plate; cover loosely with foil and let stand for 5 minutes.

In large skillet, heat ½ cup oil over high heat. Add sliced garlic and cook, stirring constantly, until golden. Add spinach to pan and cook, stirring constantly, until just limp, about 30 seconds. Remove from heat and season with lemon juice and salt and pepper to taste. Toss to coat well.

Divide spinach among 4 plates. Slice steaks into ¼-inch-thick strips and arrange on plates. Sprinkle lightly with Parmesan cheese; serve immediately.

THAI MARINATED VENISON RIBBONS

Serves: 4 ✳ Prep Time: 10 minutes ✳ Marinating Time: 4 hours ✳ Cooking Time: 15 minutes

Thank goodness for Chinese take-out! As our schedules become busier, ready-to-eat meals play a bigger role in our daily lives, and Chinese food is comfortingly similar at small take-out restaurants across the country. My experience with Chinese food began when I was still in grade school. Every Friday, Dad came home with a take-out Chinese meal. My sister and I loved to giggle over our favorite, the PuPu Platter. I can still envision Chrisi looking at me with her silly grin and snickering, "Please pass the PuPu."

As I look back on many marvelous years of Chinese food indulgence, I can appreciate its reliable convenience with my family. It's a comfort to know that all members of our household will vote "yes" when it comes to Chinese take-out as a last-minute dinner decision. The best part, however, is hearing my twelve-year-old son snicker, "Mom, please pass the PuPu."

Here's one of my favorite Asian-style venison recipes. It's quick and delicious. Serve with a salad or marinated cucumbers. Good eating!

Marinade:
- ½ cup fresh basil leaves, chopped
- ¼ cup reduced-sodium soy sauce
- 2 tablespoons crushed red pepper flakes
- 2 teaspoons sugar
- 2 teaspoons vinegar
- 1 teaspoon minced garlic

- 1 lb. boneless venison cutlets, well trimmed
- 2 tablespoons peanut oil (approx.)
- 2 cups water
- 1 cup no-salt beef broth
- 2 tablespoons reduced-sodium soy sauce
- 2 cups cooked, unseasoned ramen or cellophane noodles*
- Chopped green onions for garnish

In large zipper-style plastic bag, combine all marinade ingredients. Thinly slice venison diagonally across the grain into ¼-inch-wide strips (partially frozen meat is easier to slice). Add venison strips to bag with marinade. Seal bag well and shake until strips are thoroughly coated with marinade. Refrigerate for about 4 hours, turning bag occasionally.

Remove meat from marinade and place on paper towels to drain. Add 1 teaspoon of the oil to wok or large skillet. Heat over medium-high heat until very hot. Stir-fry venison in batches for 3 to 5 minutes per batch, transferring to warm platter as it is cooked; add additional oil as necessary for subsequent batches. When all venison has been cooked, return all to the wok. Add water, beef broth, soy sauce and pre-cooked noodles. Cook, stirring constantly, until entire mixture is heated through. Place on platter, garnish with green onions and serve immediately.

*Reserve ¼ cup of the cooking water and mix with cooked noodles to prevent them from sticking together.

It's good to note here that you don't need a wok to cook a stir-fry meal. Any large skillet–preferably one that's coated with a non-stick finish–will do. I like to use peanut oil for stir-frying, as it imparts a slightly different flavor to the meat and has a higher smoking point than regular corn oil. Watch the temperature of the oil when you're adding meat to the pan; if the oil is too hot, the meat will clump together when you begin cooking it.

* * * * * * * * *

When using fresh garlic, place the cloves on a cutting board. Place the side of a chef's knife on top of the cloves. With the palm of one hand, whack the side of the knife to crush open the clove. The peel will come off easily, and the crushed clove is ready to be chopped or added whole to your dish.

BROCCOLI-VENISON STIR-FRY

Serves: 2 ✳ Prep Time: 15 minutes ✳ Cooking Time: 10 minutes

- ½ lb. boneless venison, preferably rump or loin meat
- 1 tablespoon plus 1 teaspoon soy sauce, divided
- ½ cup peanut oil or vegetable oil, divided
- ¼ teaspoon pepper
- ½ cup no-salt beef broth
- ½ lb. fresh broccoli heads, cut into small flowerets
- ½ cup thinly sliced bok choy or celery
- ½ cup fresh chives, cut into ½-inch slices before measuring
- ¼ cup sliced water chestnuts
- ¼ cup canned baby corn ears
- Hot cooked white rice
- Fried Chinese noodles for garnish

Slice venison across the grain into very thin strips. In medium bowl, mix together 1 tablespoon of the soy sauce, 2 teaspoons of the oil and the pepper. Add venison strips and toss to coat.

In wok or large nonstick skillet, heat remaining oil over medium-high heat until hot but not smoking. Add venison strips, keeping them separated as you add them to prevent them from clumping together. Cook for 1 to 2 minutes, stirring constantly. With slotted spoon, transfer venison to paper towel–lined plate; set aside and keep warm.

Remove all but 2 tablespoons oil from wok; increase heat to high. Add remaining 1 teaspoon soy sauce, the beef broth and broccoli to wok. Cook for about 3 minutes, stirring frequently. Add bok choy, chives, water chestnuts and corn to wok; return drained venison to wok. Stir-fry for 2 minutes longer. Serve hot over a bed of white rice, with a decorative topping of fried Chinese noodles.

VENISON STEAK HEROES

Serves: 4 ✳ Prep Time: 15 minutes ✳ Cooking Time: 10 minutes

- ¼ cup A-1 Steak Sauce
- 1 tablespoon brown sugar
- 1 tablespoon soy sauce
- ½ teaspoon ground ginger
- 1 tablespoon peanut oil
- 1 lb. venison loin, cut into ½-inch strips
- 1 medium red bell pepper, thinly sliced
- 1 medium yellow bell pepper, thinly sliced
- 1 medium onion, thinly sliced
- 1 cup sliced fresh button mushrooms
- 2 cloves garlic, minced
- 4 hero rolls, split and toasted

In small saucepan, combine steak sauce, brown sugar, soy sauce and ginger. Heat over low heat, stirring constantly, until sugar dissolves. Remove from heat and set aside.

In wok or large nonstick skillet, heat oil over high heat until hot but not smoking. Add venison strips and stir-fry for about 1 minute. Add red and yellow peppers, onion, mushrooms and garlic. Stir-fry for 3 to 4 minutes. Stir in steak-sauce mixture. Cook for 5 minutes longer, stirring constantly. Spoon hot mixture onto split rolls.

Venison and Vegetable Kabobs

Serves: 4 ✳ Prep Time: 20 minutes
Marinating Time: 4 to 6 hours
Cooking Time: 10 minutes or less

Meat Marinade:

- ¾ cup olive oil
- ¼ cup red wine vinegar
- 1 tablespoon chopped fresh parsley
- 1 teaspoon cumin
- ⅛ teaspoon crumbled dried oregano, preferably Mexican
- Salt and pepper to taste
- 4 cloves garlic, chopped

- 1½ lbs. boneless venison loin or top round, well trimmed and cut into 1-inch cubes

Vegetable Marinade:

- ½ cup soy sauce
- ¼ cup sesame oil
- 2 tablespoons lemon juice
- 1 tablespoon shredded fresh gingerroot
- 5 cloves garlic, chopped

- 8 fresh button or small portobello mushrooms, cut into 1-inch chunks
- 1 large onion, cut into 1-inch chunks
- 1 red bell pepper, cut into 1-inch chunks
- 1 green bell pepper, cut into 1-inch chunks
- 1 yellow bell pepper, cut into 1-inch chunks

In large zipper-style plastic bag (or nonreactive bowl), combine all meat marinade ingredients. Add venison cubes. Seal bag well and shake until cubes are thoroughly coated with marinade. In another large zipper-style plastic bag, combine all vegetable marinade ingredients. Add mushrooms, onion and bell pepper chunks. Seal bag well and shake until vegetables are thoroughly coated with marinade. Refrigerate both bags for 4 to 6 hours, turning bags occasionally.

Bring venison and vegetables to room temperature prior to grilling. Prepare grill for high heat; light coals or preheat gas grill. Drain venison and vegetables, reserving venison marinade. Thread mushrooms, peppers, onions and venison onto metal skewers. Grill for 5 to 10 minutes, turning skewers and basting with the venison marinade several times.

CHINESE VENISON STEAK WITH MUSHROOMS

Serves: 6 ✱ Prep Time: 15 minutes ✱ Marinating Time: 30 to 60 minutes ✱ Cooking Time: 10 minutes or less

- 1½ lbs. boneless venison steak, well trimmed
- 2 tablespoons soy sauce
- 2 tablespoons sherry
- 1 tablespoon Worcestershire sauce
- 2 teaspoons cornstarch
- 1 teaspoon sugar
- 1 teaspoon sesame oil
- ½ teaspoon pepper
- ½ cup peanut oil
- ½ lb. mushrooms, quartered
- 4 scallions, cut into ½-inch lengths
- 1 can (8 oz.) whole water chestnuts, drained
- 1 package (10 oz.) frozen snow peas, thawed
- 3 tablespoons water
- 2 tablespoons sesame seeds
- Hot cooked white rice

Cut steak into 1½-inch cubes. Pound cubes with meat mallet to flatten to about ¾ inch thick. In nonreactive bowl, combine soy sauce, sherry, Worcestershire sauce, cornstarch, sugar, sesame oil and pepper. Add flattened venison, stirring to coat. Cover and refrigerate for 30 to 60 minutes.

Remove venison from marinade; discard marinade. Let venison stand until room temperature.

Set a colander inside a pot or large bowl; set aside. In wok or large nonstick skillet, heat oil over high heat until hot but not smoking. Add venison and stir-fry for about 2 minutes (if using smaller skillet, cook venison in batches). Transfer venison to colander to drain.

Remove all but 2 tablespoons oil from wok. Add mushrooms and scallions; stir-fry for 2 minutes. Add water chestnuts and snow peas; stir-fry for 30 seconds longer. Return drained venison to wok and stir well. Add water and cook for 30 seconds longer. Sprinkle venison mixture with sesame seeds. Serve immediately with hot white rice.

Gunnison Venison Goulash

Serves: 4 to 6 ✳ Prep Time: 10 minutes ✳ Marinating Time: 8 hours ✳ Cooking Time: 1¾ hours

The mountains surrounding Crawford, Colorado harbor large numbers of elk. One year, Peter and I were hunting that area during early October when the rut was in full swing. We had summited one peak, which Peter had affectionately nicknamed "Zit-Zit Mountain" (due to its propensity to be struck by lightning), and were glassing the clearing below. My heart nearly skipped a beat when I spotted a dandy 5x5 elk just on the edge of the forest. It was grazing with a harem of four cows. Peter and I planned our route to get closer to the bull and lure it in with a few seductive cow calls.

Forty minutes later, we set up behind a large fallen tree and started with a few soft mews. What happened next still sends chills down my spine. The big 5x5 lifted its head and answered with a bellowing bugle. In the middle of the bugle, from just to the elk's right, out stepped another bull, with a massive 6x5 rack. The pushing, shoving, grunting and fighting that ensued was awe-inspiring! When they finally broke, I got an opportunity to rest my gun and take one well-placed shot. The bullet from my .308 single-shot rifle put plenty of elk venison in our freezer that season. Here's one recipe that I used to take advantage of that bounty. The recipe can be doubled if you're serving a large group. Serve this with hot buttered noodles.

Marinade:

- 3 cups dry red wine
- 2 medium onions, diced
- 4 cloves garlic, crushed
- ½ teaspoon whole black peppercorns
- ¼ teaspoon crumbled dried rosemary
- ¼ teaspoon crumbled dried thyme

- 2 lbs. boneless venison stew meat (shoulder), well trimmed and cut into 1-inch cubes
- Salt and pepper
- 3 tablespoons canola oil
- 1 tablespoon flour
- 1 carrot, diced
- ¼ teaspoon cinnamon
- ¼ teaspoon cloves
- ½ cup sour cream

Combine all marinade ingredients in large nonreactive saucepan and heat to boiling. Remove from heat and let cool. Place venison cubes in marinade. Cover and refrigerate for 8 hours or overnight, stirring occasionally.

Remove the venison from the marinade; reserve marinade. Pat venison dry, and season to taste with salt and pepper. In large Dutch oven, heat oil over medium-high heat until hot but not smoking. Add venison cubes and brown on all sides, cooking in batches if necessary. Transfer venison to bowl as it is browned; set aside.

Add flour and carrot to pan. Cook over medium heat, stirring constantly, until oil is absorbed into flour, 2 to 3 minutes. Stir in reserved marinade, cinnamon, cloves and browned venison. Heat to boiling. Lower heat; cover and let simmer for about 1½ hours, or until venison is very tender. Remove venison from pan. Stir sour cream into pan juices and cook, stirring constantly, for about 5 minutes; don't let the mixture boil or the sour cream will curdle. Add salt and pepper to taste.

WILD GAME LASAGNA ITALIANO

Serves: 8 to 10 ✳ Prep Time: 1¼ hours, mostly for sauce preparation ✳ Cooking Time: 50 minutes

For those who love lasagna but prefer it without all the mozzarella cheese, this is a tasty alternative. This dish is based on a recipe from a long-time friend of Peter's who served us a delicious meal while we were fishing salmon in Alaska many years ago. It was prepared compliments of an Alaskan moose that had made its way into camp—through many feet of snow— the previous hunting season.

- 1 quantity of Venison Bolognese Sauce (below)
- 1 quantity of Béchamel Sauce (page 83)
- 1 package (16 oz.) lasagna noodles
- 1¼ cups grated Parmesan cheese

Prepare sauces according to recipe directions. While sauces are simmering, cook lasagna according to package directions; drain well. Arrange drained lasagna noodles on wax paper to prevent them from sticking together.

Heat oven to 350°F. Pour a layer of Venison Bolognese Sauce into 13x9x2-inch baking dish. Top with a layer of lasagna noodles; they should touch but not overlap. Next, top with another layer of Bolognese Sauce. Follow with a thin layer of Béchamel Sauce. Sprinkle some of the Parmesan cheese over the Béchamel.

Repeat layering order until pan is almost full, ending with a layer of Parmesan cheese. Cover with foil and bake for about 30 minutes, or until bubbly. Remove foil and bake for 10 minutes longer to lightly brown the dish. Let stand for 10 minutes before serving.

This can be assembled a day ahead and refrigerated before baking. Cover with plastic wrap, then foil. Bring to room temperature, remove plastic wrap and re-cover with foil before baking.

VENISON BOLOGNESE SAUCE

Serves: 4 ✳ Prep Time: 5 minutes ✳ Cooking Time: 1¼ hours

Serve over a bed of hot linguini, topped with freshly grated Parmesan cheese and red pepper flakes. A green salad and garlic bread go well on the side.

- 2 onions, chopped
- 3 garlic cloves, minced
- 3 tablespoons olive oil
- 1 lb. ground venison
- 1 can (28 oz.) plum tomatoes, drained and chopped
- 1 can (6 oz.) tomato paste
- 1 teaspoon salt
- ½ teaspoon pepper
- ½ teaspoon sugar
- ½ teaspoon crumbled dried oregano
- 1 bay leaf, crumbled

In large skillet, cook onions and garlic in oil over medium heat until soft. Add venison and cook until meat is no longer pink, stirring to break up. Add tomatoes and tomato paste, and simmer for about 30 minutes. Add seasonings and cook for 30 minutes longer. Remove bay leaf before serving.

MEATLOAF PARMENTIER

*Serves: 6 to 8 * Prep Time: 15 minutes * Cooking Time: 1¼ hours*

This is an easy meal to put together, because the potatoes roast in the same dish as the meatloaf. Pop in the Broccoli Casserole on page 85 for the last hour the meatloaf bakes, and you've got the entire meal in the oven at once.

- 2 lbs. ground venison
- ½ cup chopped onion
- ¼ cup minced green bell pepper
- 2 cloves garlic, minced
- 1 teaspoon salt
- ½ teaspoon cumin
- ¼ teaspoon pepper
- 2 eggs
- 3 tablespoons beef broth
- 2 tablespoons Worcestershire sauce
- 1 tablespoon green Tabasco sauce
- 2 lbs. tiny new potatoes, scrubbed but not peeled
- 2 teaspoons canola oil, optional

Heat oven to 350°F. In large bowl, mix together the venison, onion, green pepper, garlic, salt, cumin and pepper. In another bowl, beat together the eggs, broth, Worcestershire sauce and Tabasco. Pour egg mixture into meat mixture, and mix gently but thoroughly. Shape into loaf and place in roasting pan that has enough room for the potatoes as well.

Peel a narrow band around each of the potatoes; this prevents the skin from splitting during roasting. If you like crisp skins, place them around the meatloaf with no further preparation. If you like softer skins, toss potatoes with oil to lightly coat them first. Bake meatloaf and potatoes for about 1 hour. When the meatloaf is done, transfer to serving platter and let stand for about 10 minutes. If the potatoes are not quite done yet, depending upon their size, put the pan back in the oven for another 10 minutes or so.

SICILIAN VENISON BURGERS

Serves: 4 ✳ Prep Time: 10 minutes ✳ Cooking Time: 10 minutes

These burgers are a little smaller than my other burger recipes because they are not stuffed. Here, the delicious accompaniments go on top.

- 1¼ lbs. ground venison
- ⅓ cup fresh bread crumbs
- 2 oz. pitted black olives, finely chopped
- Salt and pepper
- 2 teaspoons canola oil*
- 2 teaspoons butter,* cut into 4 equal pieces
- 1 tablespoon olive oil
- 1 medium red onion, thinly sliced
- 1 clove garlic, minced
- 1 jar (10 oz.) artichoke hearts in oil, drained and chopped
- ¼ cup sun-dried tomato paste
- 1 teaspoon Italian herb blend
- 4 slices mozzarella cheese (1 oz. each)
- 4 club rolls, optional

In medium bowl, combine venison, bread crumbs, olives, and salt and pepper to taste. Mix gently but thoroughly, and shape into 4 flat patties (flat patties cook more evenly than rounded ones).

Heat broiler. In large skillet, heat canola oil over medium-high heat until hot but not smoking. Add patties and fry first side for about 3 minutes. While first side is cooking, place 1 piece of the butter on top of each patty. Flip and cook the other side for about 3 minutes.

While second side is cooking, heat olive oil in medium skillet over medium-high heat. Add onion and garlic and sauté until onion is soft. Add artichoke hearts and stir until they are warm.

Transfer patties to rack of broiler pan. Spread each patty with 1 tablespoon of the sun-dried tomato paste. Divide onion mixture into 4 even portions and spoon on top of patties. Sprinkle with herb blend. Place 1 cheese slice on top of each patty. Broil until cheese melts. Serve on club rolls, or sans bun.

If you are using ground venison with some type of fat added, ignore the oil and butter suggestions as you will have enough from the mixture for the pan-frying.

GRILLED MOOSE BURGERS

Serves: 4 ✳ Prep Time: 5 minutes ✳ Cooking Time: 10 minutes or less

When I grill burgers, I like to use a long-handled, hinged grill basket that holds four burgers at once. These racks allow you to flip the burgers without breaking them or losing them between the grill slats.

- 1½ lbs. ground moose or venison
- 8 slices bacon, cut in half
- 4 hamburger buns, split
- Salt and pepper
- Herbed Butter or Garlic Butter (both page 80) for serving

Prepare grill for medium-high heat; light coals or preheat gas grill. Shape the ground venison into 4 thick patties. Place 2 half-strips of bacon on each patty and place them, bacon-side down, in hinged grill basket. Place two more half-strips on each patty and close the basket.

Grill about 4 inches from coals until bacon is crisp and burgers are done to taste, 7 to 9 minutes per side. Remove from rack. Place on buns, season with salt and pepper and top with a pat of Herbed Butter or Garlic Butter.

GRILLED STUFFED VENISON BURGERS

Serves: 4 ✳ Prep Time: 5 minutes ✳ Cooking Time: 15 to 20 minutes

Here's a fun recipe for burgers. I like to serve them with fresh Jersey tomatoes, sans bun.

- 2 lbs. ground venison
- 1 teaspoon salt
- ¼ teaspoon pepper
- 1 small yellow onion, minced
- 2 tablespoons pickle relish
- 4 thin slices cheddar cheese
- 2 teaspoons canola oil (approx.)

Prepare grill for medium-high heat; light coals or preheat gas grill. Season venison with salt and pepper. Mix gently but thoroughly, and shape into 8 flat patties. In small bowl, combine onion and relish. Divide onion mixture evenly among 4 of the patties, spreading out but keeping away from edges. Top each with 1 cheese slice, then with remaining patties. Seal edges well with wet fingers. Lightly brush each patty with canola oil; this will prevent them from sticking. Place in hinged grill basket and grill to desired doneness, 8 to 10 minutes per side.

SAVORY DOE BURGERS

Serves: 4 ✳ Prep Time: 5 minutes ✳ Cooking Time: 15 to 20 minutes

Before beginning preparation of this recipe, bring all ingredients to cool room temperature. This will ensure even cooking of the burgers.

- 2 lbs. ground venison
- 4 slices bacon, cooked and finely crumbled
- ½ teaspoon salt
- ¼ teaspoon pepper
- 4 oz. Roquefort or blue cheese, room temperature
- Heavy cream as needed (1 to 2 tablespoons)
- 2 teaspoons canola oil (approx.)

Prepare grill for medium-high heat; light coals or preheat gas grill.* In medium bowl, combine venison, bacon, salt and pepper. Mix gently but thoroughly, and shape into 4 patties.

In another small bowl, beat cheese until it reaches a smooth consistency, adding a little cream if need be. Split each patty almost in half, as though butterflying. Place ¼ of the cheese in the middle of each patty and fold back together. Seal edges well with wet fingers.

Lightly brush each patty with canola oil; this will prevent them from sticking. Place in hinged grill basket and grill to desired doneness, 8 to 10 minutes per side.

If you prefer, you may pan-fry these burgers in a small amount of canola oil.

Venison Lasagna de Katarina

*Serves: 6 to 8 * Prep Time: 1 hour * Cooking Time: 1 hour*

Anyone who has gone deer hunting with Italians knows that hunting is but a small part of the overall experience. My Italian deer-hunting husband, Pietro, introduced me to this facet of hunting early on in our relationship.

We were hunting small game with a few of his relatives. After only an hour or so of chasing rabbits, Cousin Anthony announced it was time for a break. In perfect synchronization, shotguns were unloaded and we headed back to the vehicles. As I rounded the back of one car, I detected a peculiar odor. Just then, Cousin Guido and Uncle Nunzio popped open the trunk, and to my utter surprise, they began to unpack a feast of Italian cheeses, frutti di mare (seafood salad), prosciutto, fried calamari, baked ziti, lasagna, pasta and meatballs, and short ribs and gravy. It was the longest and most delicious lunch I've had afield!

In the tradition of my family by marriage, here's a tasty venison dish that you can prepare and freeze ahead of time to take to camp.

- 3 tablespoons olive oil
- ½ cup chopped onion
- 4 cloves garlic, minced
- 1 to 1½ lbs. ground venison
- 1 can (16 oz.) plum tomatoes, undrained
- 1 tablespoon crumbled dried basil
- 1 teaspoon crumbled dried oregano
- 1 teaspoon pepper
- ½ teaspoon salt
- ¾ lb. lasagna noodles
- ¾ lb. ricotta cheese
- ¾ lb. fresh spinach leaves, cut into bite-size bits
- ½ lb. shredded mozzarella cheese
- ½ cup grated Parmesan cheese

In large skillet, heat oil over medium heat. Add onion and garlic; cook until golden, stirring occasionally. Use slotted spoon to transfer onion and garlic to bowl; set aside. Add venison to skillet and cook until no longer pink, stirring to break up. Return onion and garlic to skillet.

Place tomatoes in food processor and pulse a few times to purée them; do not let them get foamy. Add to skillet with venison. Simmer for about 15 minutes over low heat. Add basil, oregano, pepper and salt; simmer for 20 minutes longer. While sauce is simmering, cook lasagna according to package directions; drain well. Arrange drained lasagna on wax paper to prevent them from sticking together.

Heat oven to 350°F. Pour a thin layer of the venison mixture into 13x9x2-inch baking dish. Top with a layer of lasagna noodles; they should touch but not overlap. Spoon one-third of the ricotta cheese onto noodles and spread evenly. Scatter half of the spinach over the ricotta. Sprinkle with one-third of the mozzarella and one-quarter of the Parmesan cheeses.

For the second layer, top cheeses with another layer of lasagna noodles. Spread half of the remaining meat sauce over the noodles. Spoon half of the remaining ricotta cheese over the sauce. Top with half of the remaining mozzarella, and one-third of the remaining Parmesan.

For the third layer, top cheeses with another layer of lasagna noodles. Top with remaining ricotta cheese, then with remaining spinach. Sprinkle with the remaining mozzarella cheese and half of the remaining Parmesan cheese. Top with a final layer of lasagna noodles. Spread remaining meat sauce over the noodles, and sprinkle with remaining Parmesan cheese. Bake for 30 to 45 minutes, or until browned and bubbly. Let stand for 10 to 15 minutes before serving.

This can be assembled a day ahead and refrigerated before baking. Cover with plastic wrap, then foil. Bring to room temperature, remove plastic wrap and re-cover with foil before baking. You may also freeze the assembled lasagna; thaw and bring to room temperature, remove plastic wrap, re-cover with foil and bake.

VENISON CHILI TOSTADAS

Serves: 4 ✳ Prep Time: 20 minutes ✳ Cooking Time: 20 minutes

These are fabulous when served with a pitcher of Sangria and a side of Spanish rice.

- 1 tablespoon canola oil, divided
- 1 small onion, chopped
- ¾ lb. ground venison
- 1½ teaspoons chili powder
- ½ teaspoon cumin
- ¼ teaspoon salt
- ⅛ teaspoon pepper
- ¼ cup water
- ¼ cup refried beans
- 4 flour tortillas (6 to 7 inches in diameter)
- ¼ cup shredded Monterey Jack or sharp cheddar cheese
- ¼ cup sour cream
- 1 cup shredded fresh spinach or lettuce
- 1 cup chopped tomatoes
- 1 red onion, thinly sliced and separated into rings

Heat oven to 375°F. In medium skillet, heat 1½ teaspoons of the oil over medium heat. Add onion and sauté until translucent. Add venison and cook until meat is no longer pink, stirring to break up. Drain grease. Add chili powder, cumin, salt and pepper. Mix well and cook for 1 minute longer. Add water and cook until mixture is almost dry. Add beans and mix well. Remove from heat, set aside and keep warm.

Brush tortillas lightly with the remaining 1½ teaspoons oil. Place on baking sheet and bake until crisp and golden, 8 to 10 minutes. Remove from oven.

Re-warm venison mixture if necessary; it should be hot. Divide venison mixture evenly between tortillas, spreading it evenly. Sprinkle 1 tablespoon of cheese over each. Return tortillas to oven and bake until cheese melts, about 3 to 4 minutes. Transfer tostadas to individual serving plates.

Spread 1 tablespoon sour cream in the middle of each tostada. Sprinkle shredded spinach around outside of sour cream circle. Sprinkle chopped tomatoes on top of spinach and top with red onion rings. Serve immediately.

Kate's Cooking Tips

If you've never made cabbage rolls before, here's a tip for preparing the cabbage leaves. Cut the stem off a large head of cabbage. Cut out just enough of the core so the leaves begin to separate. Gently place the head in a large pot of boiling water. Peel the leaves off as they begin to loosen. When you've peeled off enough leaves, remove the head from the water. Place the peeled leaves back in the boiling water for no more than 2 minutes. Remove and rinse under very cold water to stop the cooking. Pat dry.

VENISON-STUFFED CABBAGE

Serves: 4 ✳ Prep Time: 10 minutes ✳ Cooking Time: 1 hour

My mom used to prepare this for us using a combination of ground beef, pork and veal; she even found a good use for leftover rice with this dish. Over the years, I have prepared this with straight ground venison and even a mix of venison and ground pork. Either way, it is always a delicious, filling meal with an attractive presentation.

- 1 lb. ground venison
- ¾ cup leftover cooked white rice
- 4 tablespoons minced onion
- 2 tablespoons chopped fresh parsley
- ¼ teaspoon salt
- ⅛ teaspoon cayenne pepper
- 1 clove garlic, minced
- 8 large cabbage leaves, par-blanched (see sidebar)
- 4 teaspoons butter
- ¾ cup tomato juice, heated

Heat oven to 375°F. In medium bowl, combine venison, rice, onion, parsley, salt, cayenne and garlic; mix gently but thoroughly. Divide into 8 equal parts. Place 1 part at the base of each cabbage leaf and roll up, folding in the sides before the last turn. Secure with long wooden toothpicks.

Place rolls in buttered baking dish. Dot each roll with ½ teaspoon butter. Pour tomato juice around rolls. Cover and bake for about 50 minutes, basting with tomato juice several times; internal temperature must be above 140°F. Remove from oven and let stand for 10 minutes before serving.

Venetian Venison Pizza Pie

Serves: 4 ✳ Prep Time: 10 minutes ✳ Cooking Time: 15 minutes

A few years ago, Peter and I owned an Italian restaurant with a fine dining section in the back and a unique pizza area in the front. We introduced many new pizza toppings to the community. We served 24 different types of international pizza pies including Russian pizza (with vodka sauce and peas), Polish pizza (with Kielbasa and sauerkraut) and even the All-American Pie (with sliced franks and beans). They were a hit! One of the most popular pies was the Venetian Italian Pie. On it, we had Italian sausage and a sautéed Italian vegetable known as broccoli rabe, a bitter version of the more common broccoli. If you can't find it in your grocery store, you can substitute Chinese broccoli, which has a similar flavor. Try this version of our Italian Pizza Pie—with venison!

- 1 to 2 tablespoons olive oil
- 1 clove garlic, minced
- ½ lb. broccoli rabe, trimmed
- Dough for 1 pizza crust
- ⅓ cup tomato sauce
- 1 cup shredded mozzarella cheese
- ½ lb. venison garlic sausage or spicy venison sausage (remove casings if using links)
- 1 tablespoon grated Parmesan cheese

Heat oven to 450°F. In medium skillet, heat oil over medium-high heat. Add garlic and sauté until golden. Add broccoli rabe and sauté for 1 to 2 minutes. Transfer broccoli rabe to paper towel–lined plate; blot to remove excess oil. Chop coarsely.

Place dough on pizza pan or baking sheet, shaping to fill to edges. Spread tomato sauce over dough. Top with mozzarella cheese. Crumble sausage over the cheese. Arrange broccoli rabe evenly over all. Sprinkle with Parmesan cheese. Bake for 12 to 15 minutes.

Venison Sausage

Yield: 2¾ lbs. ✳ Prep Time: 20 minutes ✳ Processing Time: 30 minutes

- 2 lbs. venison meat, trimmed of all fat and connective tissue, cut into ½ x 3-inch pieces
- ¾ lb. unsalted pork fat, cut into ½ x 3-inch pieces
- 1 tablespoon brown sugar
- 2 teaspoons sea salt
- 1½ teaspoons crumbled dried sage
- ½ teaspoon black pepper
- ½ teaspoon hot red pepper flakes
- ½ teaspoon nutmeg
- ½ teaspoon cayenne pepper
- ¼ teaspoon crumbled dried rosemary
- ¼ teaspoon allspice

It will be easier to work with the fat and venison if they are well chilled. In large bowl, combine venison and fat cubes, tossing to mix. Chop or grind to coarse consistency. Return ground mixture to bowl. Add remaining ingredients. Mix with your hands until thoroughly combined.

Form sausage into patties, or use in bulk for pizza, casseroles, etc. Sausage should be kept refrigerated no longer than 3 days. If you make more than you will be using in that time, freeze bulk sausage or patties (layered with wax paper) immediately after chopping.

To prepare patties, pan-fry in nonstick skillet over medium heat until cooked completely through; if patties are frozen, thaw in refrigerator before cooking.

Note: When making sausage, everything must be as clean as possible. Wash your hands and equipment very carefully before you begin and again when you're finished. And because home-ground meat can harbor bacteria, wear clean plastic kitchen gloves if you have any abrasions or cuts.

SAUSAGE AND PEPPERS SKILLET

Serves: 4 ✳ Prep Time: 15 minutes ✳ Cooking Time: 30 minutes

- 1 lb. spicy venison sausage links, cut into 1-inch chunks
- 1 tablespoon canola oil, if needed
- 1 medium yellow onion, cut into 1-inch chunks
- 1 large red bell pepper, cut into 1-inch chunks
- 1 large green bell pepper, cut into 1-inch chunks
- 1 lb. small new potatoes, cut into ¾ -inch cubes
- ¾ cup water
- ⅛ teaspoon pepper

In deep skillet, cook sausage over medium heat for about 5 minutes. Remove all but 2 tablespoons fat from skillet. If you have lean sausage and don't have 2 tablespoons fat remaining, add canola oil as needed and let it heat up before proceeding.

Add onion, red and green peppers, potatoes, water and pepper to skillet. Reduce heat to low; cover and simmer for 20 to 25 minutes or until potatoes are tender, stirring occasionally.

Note: For a special presentation, serve in roasted red peppers. Cut off stems of peppers and remove seeds. Place under broiler for 5 to 7 minutes to blacken peppers while vegetables are simmering.

NEW YEAR'S EVE RACK OF VENISON RIBS

Serves: 4 * Prep Time: 45 minutes * Cooking Time: 40 minutes

The winter holiday season is my favorite time to prepare wild game. At that time of year, I have a wide variety of venison to choose from and plenty of opportunities to prepare decorative and festive-looking wild-game dishes for family and friends.

My family's traditional meal for New Year's Eve was laden with all kinds of seafood—breaded, fried or swimming in aromatic tomato sauce. One year, however, I decided to experiment with a venison dish for the main course. Keeping with tradition, I prepared an appetizer dish with an assortment of fishes and let everyone wonder what I was going to present for the main dish.

While the venison was cooking in the oven, the piquant aroma permeated the house and I could see the anticipation growing—or was it that I heard stomachs growling!? Scrumptious is hardly the word for this mouth-watering dish, which was such a hit that we have made it an annual tradition since. I always serve this with the Rummied Sweet Potato Casserole on page 88; green peas with pearl onions add a splash of color.

* 2 racks of venison ribs (about 8 ribs each)
* 4 cups cubed white bread (you might need a little more)
* 2 cups heavy cream (you might need a little more)
* 3 tablespoons Dijon mustard
* 2 tablespoons chopped fresh parsley
* 2 tablespoons snipped fresh chives
* 2 tablespoons chopped garlic
* 1 tablespoon prepared horseradish
* Salt and pepper

Heat oven to 350°F. "French" the ribs by trimming away the scant amount of meat that surrounds the tips of the rib bones. Trim and discard all fat from the ribs as well. Cover rib tips with foil to prevent burning. Combine bread cubes, cream, mustard, parsley, chives, garlic, horseradish, and salt and pepper to taste in food processor. Process until mixture is soft and smooth. It should be neither runny nor too firm; add a little additional bread or cream as necessary to adjust texture. Coat meat side of ribs with the mixture.* Place ribs in a single layer, coating-side up, in baking dish. Bake for 30 to 40 minutes, or until internal temperature reaches about 125°F. Remove foil from rib tips. Cut ribs into portions and serve with pan juices.

Because venison is such lean meat, the coating must cover the meat side of the ribs completely to ensure that the heat does not dry out the meat. The coating will impart a delicious seasoning to the meat as well.

BAKED MOOSE ALE RIBS

Serves: 4 * Prep Time: 10 minutes * Marinating Time: 24 hours * Cooking Time: 2 to 2½ hours

* 4 lbs. moose ribs
* Spicy Beer Marinade (page 77)

Trim and discard all outer fat from ribs. Place ribs and marinade in large plastic container or large zipper-style plastic bag. Cover or seal, and refrigerate for 24 hours, turning ribs occasionally.

Heat oven to 275°F. Place ribs and sauce in shallow roasting pan or 9x13-inch baking dish (choose a pan that will hold ribs in single layer). Cover pan with foil and bake for 2 to 2½ hours, until the venison begins to fall off the bone.

venison for breakfast

For most hunters, dinner is the meal that includes venison. Some get adventurous and plan a lunch or two with the delectable meat. However, over the years, I have discovered that venison also lends itself to many recipes for delicious breakfast meals.

I first discovered this while whitetail hunting with Peter from a remote campsite in Montana. The guide woke us in preparation for the morning's hunt and suggested we come to breakfast in clothes other than our hunting garments—a tactic we had long adhered to anyway. But when we got to the cook tent, we soon discovered why the guide was so emphatic about his suggestion. As we entered the tent, our noses were pleasantly assaulted with the pungent aroma of patty and link sausages cooking on the grill. Next to the frying sausages was a mound of cooked ground venison mixed with minced onions, hash-brown potatoes and diced green peppers. The cook gave this aromatic venison concoction a generous sprinkle of cayenne pepper and welcomed us to breakfast! I never forgot how wonderful that cooking venison smelled and how delicious breakfast was that morning.

From that point on, I have enjoyed including venison as part of our breakfast meals. Over the years, I have gotten creative with ways to incorporate all types of venison, including moose, caribou, deer, antelope and especially wild boar and javelina. For truly aromatic, delicious and easy-to-make meals, try adding venison to your breakfast schedule.

Following are some of my breakfast recipes I have shared with our family and friends. Enjoy these with some savory, fresh-baked rolls or toasted English muffins and hot fresh coffee.

Venison Vegetable Frittata

Serves: 6 ✳ Prep Time: 15 minutes ✳ Cooking Time: 30 minutes

Frittatas are ideal dishes for spring and summer because they're light and they cook quickly. I tasted my first frittata at a Mama Lucci's restaurant in the Little Italy section of New York City many years ago. It was a hot summer's day, and the lunchtime crowd had packed the air-conditioned bistros. Peter and I decided to take a sidewalk seat instead and do the "New York" thing—people-watching while enjoying a light meal.

I started making this dish a few years ago to change up our summer brunches. It's perfect when we've had an early rise to start working in the yard and have skipped a good breakfast. Serve it with a side of salsa and fresh-baked biscuits.

- ½ lb. ground venison
- Salt, black pepper and cayenne pepper
- ¼ cup unsalted butter, divided
- 3 tablespoons minced shallots
- 1 tablespoon minced garlic
- 1 lb. fresh button mushrooms, sliced
- ½ cup diced fresh zucchini
- 8 eggs, room temperature
- ½ lb. fresh spinach leaves, torn or finely chopped
- 1 cup small-curd cottage cheese
- ¼ cup grated Parmesan cheese
- 1 tablespoon olive oil

Cook venison in large skillet over medium heat until no longer pink, stirring to break up. Season to taste with salt, black pepper and cayenne pepper; set aside.

In large omelet pan (minimum 12 inches), melt 2 tablespoons of the butter over medium heat. Add shallots and garlic and cook for about 3 minutes. Add mushrooms and zucchini. Sauté until liquid from the mushrooms has evaporated. Remove from heat and set aside to cool.

Heat broiler. Beat eggs in large bowl. Mix in spinach, cottage cheese and cooled venison mixture. Add the cooled mushroom mixture and stir until well combined.

Set omelet pan over medium-high heat. Melt remaining 2 tablespoons butter. Add egg mixture; as it begins to set, shake the pan to ensure it does not stick. Turn heat to low. Without stirring, continue cooking for about 10 minutes, checking to make sure the eggs to do not stick to the pan.

When egg mixture is almost completely set, sprinkle Parmesan cheese and drizzle oil on top of the frittata. Place pan under the broiler to melt the cheese; be careful not to over-cook. Slide frittata onto serving platter; cut into 6 portions.

Venison Asparagus Delight

Serves: 1 * Prep Time: 15 minutes * Cooking Time: 10 minutes

Peter created a version of this recipe over 20 years ago. In fact, he won first place in the men's division of a cooking contest with his formula. Over the years, I've adapted it to include venison and I usually prepare this egg dish when there is some leftover venison roast, steak or medallions. Serve with hot French bread and quartered fresh tomatoes.

- 1 slice uncooked bacon, chopped
- ¼ lb. leftover venison, chopped
- 2 eggs
- Dash of Tabasco sauce
- Salt and pepper
- 2 tablespoons butter
- 2 small stalks asparagus, cooked and chopped*
- ¼ cup shredded mozzarella cheese

In medium omelet pan, cook bacon over medium heat. When it is almost done, add venison and cook for 1 to 2 minutes to warm it up. Transfer venison mixture to a dish and wipe the skillet clean.

In small bowl, combine eggs, Tabasco, and salt and pepper to taste. Beat gently with fork until just blended; over-beating will make the omelet rubbery. Melt butter in cleaned omelet pan over medium-high heat. When butter begins to sizzle, add egg mixture, tilting pan to spread eggs over bottom; lower heat to medium. As soon as the eggs begin to set on the bottom, pull cooked egg from the edge with a wooden spoon and tilt the pan to let the liquid egg flow into the space. Continue to cook and repeat the last step until most of the liquid egg has been cooked.

Sprinkle cooked venison mixture over one half of the omelet. Top venison mixture with asparagus and cheese. Tilt the omelet pan to one side and fold over the "empty" half of the omelet with a spatula. To make sure all the cheese has melted, place a lid on the pan for 20 to 30 seconds. Remove the cover and transfer omelet to individual plate.

You may substitute canned asparagus for the fresh cooked asparagus, but it is not as tasty.

Simple Venison Omelet

Serves: 2 * Prep Time: 5 minutes * Cooking Time: 15 minutes

Omelets were one of the first dishes I mastered as short-order cook at the Ebb Tide in Boothbay Harbor, Maine. This restaurant was the local favorite for its fresh-baked blueberry muffins and super-size omelets. This quick venison omelet will fill bellies with warm satisfaction!

- 2 slices uncooked bacon, chopped
- ⅓ lb. ground venison
- 4 eggs
- 2 tablespoons water, divided
- Salt and pepper
- 1 tablespoon butter (approx., depending on size of omelet pan), divided
- ½ cup shredded cheddar cheese, divided

In medium omelet pan, cook bacon over medium heat. When it is almost done, add venison and cook for 1 to 2 minutes to warm it up. Transfer venison mixture to a dish and wipe the skillet clean.

In small bowl, combine 2 of the eggs, 1 tablespoon water, and salt and pepper to taste. Beat gently with fork until just blended; over-beating will make the omelet rubbery. Melt 1 to 1½ teaspoons of the butter in cleaned omelet pan over medium-high heat. When butter begins to sizzle, add egg mixture, tilting pan to spread eggs over bottom; lower heat to medium. As soon as the eggs begin to set on the bottom, pull cooked egg from the edge with a wooden spoon and tilt the pan to let the liquid egg flow into the space. Continue to cook and repeat the last step until most of the liquid egg has been cooked.

Sprinkle half of the cooked venison mixture and half of the cheese over one half of the omelet. Tilt the omelet pan to one side and fold over the "empty" half of the omelet with a spatula. To make sure all the cheese has melted, place a lid on the pan for 20 to 30 seconds. Remove the cover and transfer omelet to individual plate. Cook the second omelet in the same manner as the first.

Venison Asparagus Delight

pies & casseroles

The group I hunt with and cook for in deer camp raves about my wild-game dishes. But sometimes they can be very uncreative. Whenever I ask what special dish I can make for them, they come up with the same three requests.

One is a venison casserole that they have named Kate's Deer Camp Casserole. It's one of the simplest dishes I make (see recipe on p. 64). It contains whole corn kernels, chopped broccoli flowerets, cooked ground venison, some onion soup mix, sour cream and a few simple spices, and it is served over a bed of hot buttered egg noodles.

Two years ago, knowing the guys like to eat this meal at least twice during the first week of deer camp, I prepared enough of this dish to feed the 12 people we had in camp three different times during the week. On Sunday, as we were packing to leave, I asked if anyone wanted to take some of the venison leftovers home. Even though there were some very delicious dishes left, there were a bunch of sour faces because there weren't any Deer Camp Casserole leftovers! Sometimes you just can't win.

When you need to put a delicious meal on the table with minimal fuss, turn to these recipes, as I often do. They're great for family-style meals, and most also work well in deer camp. Not only are they appetizing, but they provide a complete, balanced meal in a single dish.

LEFTOVER VENISON POT PIE

Serves: 4 ✳ Prep Time: 20 minutes ✳ Cooking Time: 30 minutes

- 4 slices bacon, chopped
- 1 medium onion, chopped
- 1 lb. leftover cooked venison roast or steak, cut into bite-size pieces
- 1½ cups gravy (leftover or canned)
- 1 package (10 oz.) frozen sliced carrots, thawed and drained
- 1½ cups frozen hash-brown potatoes, thawed
- ½ cup drained canned straw mushrooms
- ½ teaspoon crumbled dried marjoram
- Salt and pepper
- Pastry dough for 1-crust pie (purchased or homemade), rolled out

Heat oven to 425°F. Lightly grease a shallow casserole that measures about 8 inches across the top; set aside. In medium skillet, cook bacon over medium heat until crisp. Remove bacon with slotted spoon; set aside. Reserve 3 tablespoons bacon fat in skillet.

Add onion to bacon fat in skillet and cook until soft, stirring occasionally. Return cooked bacon to skillet; add venison, gravy, carrots, potatoes, mushrooms, marjoram, and salt and pepper to taste. Cook, stirring constantly, until mixture begins to simmer. Transfer mixture to prepared casserole. Center pie crust on top of casserole. Crimp edges and cut 3 or 4 small vents on top. Bake for about 20 minutes, or until bubbly. If crust begins to brown too much, cover loosely with foil. Let stand for 10 minutes before serving.

Note: You may also prepare 4 individual pies, using 3-inch pie tins.

Kate's Cooking Tips

To ensure that pie crust does not become too soggy when baked, prepare the dough ahead of time. Line the pan with the rolled dough and place it in the refrigerator while you prepare other parts of the recipe.

• • • • • • • • •

Anaheim peppers are a fresh green chile with a little more heat than a green bell pepper. If you can't find Anaheim peppers in your market, substitute chopped green bell pepper with a little jalapeño pepper thrown in for heat. On the other hand, if you prefer really spicy food, use 2 tablespoons chopped Anaheim peppers and 2 tablespoons chopped jalapeño peppers.

VENISON TAMALE PIE

Serves: 6 ✳ Prep Time: 20 minutes ✳ Cooking Time: 40 minutes

Here's a dish that takes a little bit of extra time because of the cornmeal crust. But it's well worth the effort! It was during a whitetail hunting trip to south Texas that I first tasted true tamales. We were hunting at the Lazy Fork Ranch and the cook prepared many dishes native to her Mexican homeland. Although I wasn't able to get the exact recipe from her, this one comes close—and I haven't had any complaints on the receiving end when I serve it!

Filling

* 1 tablespoon canola oil
* 1 lb. ground venison
* 4 scallions, chopped
* 1 can (8 oz.) tomato sauce
* 1 cup whole-kernel corn, drained
* ¼ cup chopped Anaheim peppers (for more zing, use a blend of Anaheim and jalapeño peppers)
* ¼ cup cornmeal
* 1 teaspoon chili powder
* 1 teaspoon salt
* ½ teaspoon pepper
* ½ teaspoon cumin
* ¼ teaspoon crumbled dried oregano leaves

Cornmeal Pie Crust

* 1 cup all-purpose flour, plus additional for rolling out crust
* 2 tablespoons cornmeal
* ⅓ cup vegetable shortening
* 3 to 4 tablespoons cold water

Topping

* 1 egg, lightly beaten
* ¼ cup evaporated milk
* ½ teaspoon dry mustard
* 1 cup shredded Monterey Jack cheese
* 1 cup shredded cheddar cheese
* 6 pitted black olives, sliced

Sour cream and chopped tomatoes for garnish, optional

Heat oven to 425°F.

To prepare filling: In large skillet, heat oil over medium heat. Add venison and cook until no longer pink, stirring to break up. Drain. Mix in remaining filling ingredients. Let simmer for 5 minutes, then remove from heat.

To prepare crust: In small bowl, blend together flour and cornmeal. Cut in shortening with pastry blender or two knives. When mixture resembles coarse meal or very small peas, add water a little at a time, mixing with fork until dough is formed. Roll out pastry on floured surface until it forms a 15-inch circle. Fit pastry into deep-dish 9-inch pie pan and crimp edges.

Spoon filling into pie crust. Place pie pan on baking sheet and bake for 25 minutes. While it is baking, prepare the topping for the pie: Combine egg, milk and mustard in medium bowl; mix well. When pie has baked for 25 minutes, remove from oven, sprinkle cheeses over filling and pour milk mixture on top. Decorate with sliced olives. Return to oven and bake for an additional 5 minutes. Let stand for 10 minutes before serving. Serve with sour cream and chopped tomatoes.

VENISON-BARLEY CASSEROLE

Serves: 4 ✳ Prep Time: 20 minutes ✳ Cooking Time: 45 minutes

- 1 large onion, minced
- 2 cloves garlic, minced
- 1/2 cup finely chopped green bell pepper
- 1 tablespoon canola oil
- 1 lb. ground venison
- 12 oz. fresh mushrooms, thinly sliced
- 2 cups beef broth
- 2 cups water
- 8 oz. pearl barley, rinsed and drained
- 4 carrots, peeled and thinly sliced
- 4 stalks celery, thinly sliced
- 1 bay leaf
- 1 teaspoon salt
- 1/2 teaspoon dehydrated parsley flakes
- 1/4 teaspoon pepper
- 1/8 teaspoon nutmeg

In stockpot or Dutch oven, sauté onion, garlic and pepper in oil over medium-high heat. When onions are soft, add venison and cook until meat is no longer pink, stirring to break up. Add mushrooms; cook for about 5 minutes longer. Add remaining ingredients. Cover, reduce heat to low and simmer for about 30 minutes. Uncover and check the tenderness of the barley. Continue cooking until most of the liquid is absorbed and barley is tender, about 10 to 15 minutes longer. Remove bay leaf before serving.

QUICK VENISON CHILI PIE

❧

*Serves: 6 * Prep Time: 15 minutes * Cooking Time: 25 minutes*

- 2 tablespoons canola oil, divided
- 1 lb. ground venison
- 1 cup chopped onion
- ¼ cup chopped green or red bell pepper
- 1 can (8 oz.) tomato sauce
- ½ cup cooked kidney beans
- 1 tablespoon chili powder
- ¼ teaspoon salt
- 1 cup shredded cheddar cheese
- 2 tablespoons chopped jalapeño peppers
- 1 cup milk
- 2 eggs
- ½ cup buttermilk baking mix
- Sour cream and chopped tomatoes for garnish, optional

Heat oven to 375°F. Lightly grease deep-dish 9-inch pie pan; set aside. In large skillet, heat 1 tablespoon of the oil over medium heat. Add venison and cook until no longer pink, stirring to break up. Transfer venison to medium bowl; set aside.

Heat remaining tablespoon oil in same skillet over medium heat. Add onion and pepper and sauté until onions are soft. Add tomato sauce, beans, chili powder and salt, stirring to blend. Return venison to skillet and stir for about a minute to mix thoroughly.

Pour meat mixture in prepared pie pan. Sprinkle with cheese and jalapeños. In small bowl, combine milk and eggs; beat with fork. Add baking mix; stir until just combined. Pour over the cheese topping. Bake for 20 to 25 minutes, or until top is golden. Serve with sour cream and chopped tomatoes.

VENISON MOUSSAKA

❧

*Serves: 6 * Prep Time: 1 hour * Cooking Time: 55 minutes*

My first introduction to genuine Greek food was while I was attending Cornell University's Hotel School. The school's dining facility offered a wide variety of foods every day. Since many of the students came from different countries, the staff created meals native to the students' homelands. What a treat! It was in the Ratskellar (or "Rat Cellar," as we affectionately called it) where I first tasted moussaka made with ground lamb. Since then, I've experimented with several recipes to create Venison Moussaka—one of our household favorites.

- 1 medium eggplant, peeled and sliced into ½-inch-thick rounds
- Salt
- 6 tablespoons olive oil, divided
- ¼ cup chopped onion
- 2 cloves garlic, minced
- 1 lb. ground venison
- ½ teaspoon crumbled dried oregano
- ½ teaspoon salt
- ½ teaspoon freshly ground black pepper
- 1 can (8 oz.) tomato sauce
- 3 eggs
- 2 cups light cream
- 1 cup ricotta cheese
- 2 tablespoons minced fresh parsley
- 1 cup dry bread crumbs, divided
- ¼ cup butter, melted

Heat oven to 350°F. Lightly grease 13x9x2-inch baking dish; set aside. Lightly grease large baking sheet and arrange eggplant slices in single layer. Sprinkle lightly with salt. Bake, uncovered, for about 15 minutes, or until tender. Transfer eggplant to prepared baking dish, overlapping slices slightly; set aside. Reduce oven to 325°F.

In large skillet, heat 2 tablespoon of the oil over medium-high heat. Add onion and garlic, and sauté until onions are soft. Add venison and cook until meat is no longer pink, stirring to break up. Reduce heat to low. Add oregano, salt, pepper and tomato sauce to skillet, stirring to combine. Simmer for about 20 minutes. Remove from heat and set aside.

In medium bowl, combine eggs, cream, ricotta cheese, parsley and ¼ cup of the bread crumbs. Beat well until smooth.

Spread meat mixture over eggplant in baking dish. Pour egg mixture evenly over the top. Sprinkle remaining ¾ cup bread crumbs on top; drizzle butter on top of bread crumbs. Bake, uncovered, for 45 minutes, or until bubbly. Let stand at room temperature for about 10 minutes before serving.

DEER CAMP CASSEROLE

❧

Serves: 4 ✳ Prep Time: 10 minutes ✳ Cooking Time: 45 minutes

- 2 medium onions, chopped
- 1 tablespoon canola oil
- 1 lb. ground venison
- 1 envelope Lipton's onion-mushroom soup mix
- 1 cup hot water
- 1 tablespoon chopped fresh parsley
- 1/2 teaspoon pepper
- 1 can (11 oz.) whole-kernel corn, drained
- 1 cup chopped broccoli flowerets
- 1 cup dairy sour cream
- 1 can (2.8 oz.) French-fried onions
- Hot cooked noodles, optional

Heat oven to 350°F. In large skillet, sauté onions in oil over medium-high heat until soft. Add venison and cook until meat is no longer pink, stirring to break up.

In measuring cup or small bowl, stir together soup mix and hot water. Add soup mixture, parsley and pepper to venison; mix well. Remove from heat. Add corn, broccoli and sour cream, and mix thoroughly. Transfer to medium casserole. Sprinkle with French-fried onions. Cover and bake for 30 minutes. Uncover and bake for 15 minutes longer. Serve over a bed of hot buttered egg noodles.

CHILI CASSEROLE

✄

Serves: 4 ✳ Prep Time: 15 minutes ✳ Cooking Time: 1 1/4 hours

- 4 slices bacon, chopped
- 1 cup chopped onion
- 1/4 cup chopped green bell pepper
- 1 lb. ground venison
- 1 can (15 oz.) kidney beans, drained
- 1 can (11 oz.) whole-kernel corn, drained
- 1 cup chopped canned tomatoes, drained before chopping
- 2 tablespoons tomato paste
- 2 teaspoons chili powder
- 1/2 teaspoon salt
- 3 cloves garlic, minced
- Hot cooked white rice and shredded cheddar cheese for serving, optional

Heat oven to 300°F. In large skillet, cook bacon over medium heat until just crisp, stirring occasionally. Add onion and green pepper to skillet; cook until tender, stirring occasionally. Add venison and cook until meat is no longer pink, stirring to break up. Remove from heat; set aside.

In medium bowl, combine remaining ingredients except rice and cheese; toss well to combine. Add to meat mixture and stir well. Transfer to medium casserole or glass baking dish. Cover and bake for 1 hour 10 minutes. Serve with hot rice and shredded cheddar cheese.

EGGPLANT-VENISON CASSEROLE

☘

Serves: 6 ✳ Prep Time: 20 minutes ✳ Cooking Time: 45 minutes

- 1 tablespoon olive oil
- 2 lbs. ground venison
- 1 medium onion, chopped
- 1 small green bell pepper, cored and chopped
- 1 tablespoon all-purpose flour
- 1 teaspoon crumbled dried oregano
- 1/2 teaspoon pepper
- 1/2 teaspoon salt
- 2 cups tomato sauce
- 1 large eggplant, peeled and sliced into 1/2-inch-thick rounds
- 1 cup shredded mozzarella cheese, divided

Heat oven to 325°F. Lightly grease 2-quart casserole; set aside. Heat oil in large skillet over medium-high heat. Add venison and cook until no longer pink, stirring to break up. With slotted spoon, transfer venison to bowl; set aside.

Add onion and pepper to skillet and sauté until soft. Return venison to skillet. Stir in the flour, oregano, pepper, salt and tomato sauce. Reduce heat and simmer for about 10 minutes.

Meanwhile, arrange half of the eggplant slices in prepared casserole. When meat mixture is ready, spoon half of it over eggplant. Top with half of the cheese, then layer remaining eggplant, followed with remaining meat mixture. Top with remaining cheese. Cover and bake for 45 minutes.

BAKED ZITI WITH VENISON

Serves: 4 * Prep Time: 25 minutes * Cooking Time: 35 minutes

A loaf of savory Italian garlic bread makes a great accompaniment to this dish. If you have cooked ziti on hand, preparation time is reduced to 10 minutes ... quick and easy!

- 8 oz. uncooked ziti pasta
- ½ cup finely chopped onion
- 3 cloves garlic, minced
- 2 tablespoons canola oil
- 1 cup chopped broccoli
- 1 lb. ground venison
- ½ teaspoon crumbled dried oregano
- ½ teaspoon salt
- ¼ teaspoon black pepper
- ¼ teaspoon hot red pepper flakes
- 1 can (8 oz.) tomato sauce
- 1 cup canned mushrooms, undrained
- 2 cups shredded mozzarella cheese
- ½ cup grated Parmesan cheese

Heat oven to 350°F. Prepare ziti according to package directions. Drain; set aside.

In large skillet, sauté onion and garlic in oil over medium-high heat until softened; do not let garlic brown. Add broccoli and sauté for 3 to 5 minutes longer. Add venison, oregano, salt, black pepper and red pepper flakes. Cook until venison is no longer pink, stirring to break up meat. Mix in tomato sauce and mushrooms with their liquid. Heat to a simmer. Add cooked ziti and mix well. Transfer mixture to shallow casserole. Sprinkle both cheeses on top and bake, uncovered, for 35 minutes, or until mixture bubbles and cheese is lightly browned.

soups, stews & chilies

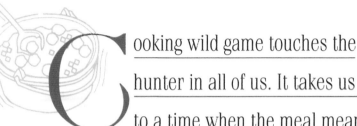

Cooking wild game touches the hunter in all of us. It takes us back to a time when the meal meant not only the gathering of family and friends around the table, but also their survival.

I can easily understand how our ancestors had to utilize every cut of meat, tender or tough, that they brought home. The less-prime cuts are perfect for soups, stews and chilies; the long, slow cooking tenderizes tough meats and squeezes out every drop of flavor. And what can be more welcoming than the down-home aroma of a pot of venison, with savory vegetables and spices, slowly simmering on the stove?

In modern days, these recipes also provide a link to the past. My grandmother told me about her grandmother's and her grandmother's mother's recipes for savory pot meals. I, too, have created recipes for these dishes that I hope will be passed down. Easy to prepare, flavorful and most of all rib-sticking and filling, these soups, stews and chilies will be loved by all you serve them to.

VENISON MINESTRONE SOUP

Serves: 8 ✳ Prep Time: 30 minutes ✳ Cooking Time: 1½ hours

- ½ cup all-purpose flour
- Salt and pepper
- 1 lb. venison stew meat, cut into ½-inch cubes
- 2 tablespoons olive oil, divided
- 3 medium onions, chopped
- 3 stalks celery, chopped
- 3 cloves garlic, minced
- 2 tablespoons chopped fresh parsley
- 2 cans (14½ oz. each) beef broth
- 1 can (6 oz.) tomato paste
- 3 beef bouillon cubes
- ½ to ¾ lb. carrots, peeled and cut into rounds
- 1 teaspoon salt
- ½ teaspoon crumbled dried rosemary
- ½ teaspoon pepper
- ⅛ teaspoon ground sage
- 2 quarts water
- 1 cup cooked macaroni (al dente)
- 1 can (15 oz.) kidney beans, drained
- 1 zucchini, chopped or thinly sliced
- ½ lb. fresh or thawed frozen green beans
- Grated Parmesan cheese for garnish

Place flour in large plastic food-storage bag; add salt and pepper to taste and shake well to mix. Add cubed venison and toss to coat. In large skillet, heat 1 tablespoon of the oil over medium-high heat until it is hot but not smoking. Brown floured venison cubes in small batches and transfer to a plate as it is browned. Set aside.

In stockpot or Dutch oven, sauté the onion, celery, garlic and parsley in the remaining tablespoon of the oil over medium heat. Add broth, tomato paste, bouillon cubes, carrots, salt, rosemary, pepper, sage and water. Heat to boiling. Add browned venison. Reduce heat, cover and simmer for about 1 hour, stirring frequently. Add macaroni, kidney beans, zucchini and green beans and simmer for about 30 minutes longer. Before serving, garnish with Parmesan cheese.

Escarole Soup with Venison Meat-a-Balls

Serves: 6 ✴ Prep Time: 15 minutes ✴ Cooking Time: 45 minutes

My husband's Italian mother, Lucy, introduced me to many different foodstuffs—escarole, broccoli rabe, scungilli and calamari, to name a few. She often reminded me about the way many Italian dishes are prepared: "Use garlic, garlic and more garlic." Both her escarole and broccoli rabe dishes started by sautéeing plenty of garlic; the greens were added as the garlic was cooking. After this, chicken broth was added to finish cooking the greens.

When I shared with her this venison version of her Meatball Escarole Soup, she was quite pleased, and I was happy that I had passed her test. Then she cautiously whispered in my ear, "But next time, use a little more garlic!"

- ½ cup bread crumbs
- ½ cup milk
- 1 lb. ground venison
- 1 egg, beaten
- 2 tablespoons grated Parmesan cheese, plus additional for serving
- 1 tablespoon chopped fresh parsley
- 7 cloves garlic, minced, divided
- Salt and pepper
- 3 tablespoons olive oil
- 1 lb. escarole, washed and chopped
- 4 cans (14½ oz. each) chicken broth
- Italian bread for accompaniment, optional

In medium bowl, mix together bread crumbs and milk; let stand for about 5 minutes. Add venison, egg, Parmesan cheese, parsley, half of the garlic, and salt and pepper to taste. Mix well. Shape into small meatballs (small enough to fit on a spoon and pop into your mouth) and place on a plate. Cover and refrigerate while you prepare the rest of the soup mixture.

In large saucepot or Dutch oven, heat oil over medium-high heat. Add remaining garlic and sauté until golden; do not let it brown. Stir in escarole and continue sautéeing until escarole has wilted down. Add chicken broth. Cover pot and simmer for about 30 minutes. Gently add meatballs to the simmering broth. Leave them untouched for a few minutes so they can set, then stir gently and continue simmering for 7 to 10 minutes longer, until the meatballs are cooked through. I always sample a meatball at about 7 minutes to see if it's done yet.

Serve hot, with plenty of grated Parmesan cheese and Italian bread.

Venison Onion Soup

Serves: 5 ✳ Prep Time: 20 minutes ✳ Cooking Time: 1 hour

Onions have a multitude of delicious uses: frying, sautéeing, stuffing, simmering in soups and baking. The most common variety, the yellow onion, has a flavor that stands up to all types of cooking, and it adds a golden color to dishes. Large white Bermuda or flat Spanish red onions are milder than the yellow and are good raw on burgers. Scallions are often used in soups for flavoring, as in this delicious soup du jour. What could be better than a delicious combination of venison and onions at the end of the day? This soup is good served with hot crescent rolls.

- 1 cup all-purpose flour
- Salt and pepper
- 1½ lbs. boneless venison, cut into 1-inch cubes
- 3 tablespoons canola oil (approx.), divided
- 5 medium yellow onions, chopped
- 2 bunches scallions, chopped
- ¼ lb. celery, chopped
- ¼ lb. carrots, cut lengthwise into halves then sliced into half-rounds
- 2 cups beef stock
- 2 cups V8 juice
- ¾ cup canned crushed tomatoes with their juices
- 2 cups water
- Pepper and garlic salt

Place flour in large plastic food-storage bag; add salt and pepper to taste and shake well to mix. Add cubed venison and toss to coat. In Dutch oven, heat 2 tablespoons of the oil over medium-high heat until it is hot but not smoking. Brown floured venison cubes in small batches, adding additional oil as necessary, and transfer to a plate as it is browned.

Once all venison has been browned, return all cubes to Dutch oven and lower heat to medium. Add onion and sauté for about 3 minutes. Add scallions, celery and carrots; sauté for 5 minutes longer. Stir in stock, V8 juice, tomatoes and water; season to taste with pepper and garlic salt. Cover and heat to boiling. Reduce heat and simmer for about 1 hour, stirring occasionally.

It's a Meal Venison Soup

Serves: 12 ✳ Prep Time: 20 minutes ✳ Cooking Time: 3¼ hours

- 1 cup all-purpose flour
- Salt and pepper
- 2½ lbs. boneless venison, cut into ½-inch cubes
- 2 tablespoons olive oil, divided
- 1 large onion, chopped
- 1 large green bell pepper, chopped
- 3 cloves garlic, minced
- 1 can (14½ oz.) green beans, drained
- 1 can (14½ oz.) whole-kernel corn, drained
- 1 can (15¼ oz.) lima beans, drained
- 3 cans (8 oz. each) tomato sauce
- ½ lb. carrots, diced
- 1 tablespoon plus 1½ teaspoons Worcestershire sauce
- 1 teaspoon green Tabasco sauce
- 1 teaspoon crumbled dried basil
- ¼ teaspoon salt
- 3½ quarts water
- 3 large potatoes, cubed
- ½ cup chopped cabbage
- 1 can (13¼ oz.) sliced mushrooms, drained
- 2 cups uncooked elbow macaroni
- 2 tablespoons chopped fresh parsley

Place flour in large plastic food-storage bag; add salt and pepper to taste and shake well to mix. Add cubed venison and toss to coat. In large skillet, heat 1 tablespoon of the oil over medium-high heat until it is hot but not smoking. Brown floured venison cubes in small batches and transfer to a plate. Set aside.

In large stockpot or Dutch oven, heat the remaining tablespoon of the oil over medium-high heat. Add onion, pepper and garlic and sauté until soft. Add browned venison, green beans, corn, lima beans, tomato sauce, carrots, Worcestershire sauce, Tabasco sauce, basil, salt and water to pot. Cover and heat to boiling. Reduce heat and simmer for 2 hours, stirring occasionally. Add potatoes, cabbage and mushrooms and simmer for 30 minutes longer. Add macaroni and simmer until macaroni is tender, about 30 minutes longer. Serve hot, garnished with chopped parsley.

VENISON MEATBALL STEW

Serves: 4 ✳ Prep Time: 40 minutes ✳ Cooking Time: 45 minutes

I remember one particularly severe winter here on the East Coast. By early February we were hit by our 13th official snowstorm of the season. During this particular "Sweetheart's Month," Peter spent plenty of time outside plowing the driveway and clearing snow off outbuildings, cars and ornamental shrubbery. I spent much of the time inside keeping one eye on him, the other on our young son, Cody, while preparing savory, warm venison meals. One of my sweetheart's favorite meals is Venison Meatball Stew. Even though the meatballs and vegetables are hearty and savory, it's knowing how good a piece of buttered Italian bread will taste after it has been dunked into the sauce that puts this recipe on my "A" list. Enjoy!

Meatballs

- 1 lb. ground venison
- ¾ cup Italian-seasoned bread crumbs
- 2 tablespoons chopped fresh parsley
- 1 tablespoon minced garlic
- 1 teaspoon salt
- ¼ teaspoon crumbled dried oregano
- ¼ teaspoon pepper
- 1 egg, lightly beaten
- Olive oil as needed

Stew Ingredients

- 1 tablespoon olive oil
- ½ cup chopped onion
- ½ cup chopped green bell pepper
- ½ teaspoon chopped garlic
- 1 can (14½ oz.) plum tomatoes, undrained
- 2 cans (8 oz. each) tomato sauce
- ¼ teaspoon crumbled dried oregano
- ¼ teaspoon cumin
- ¼ teaspoon pepper
- ¾ lb. zucchini, peeled and sliced into ½-inch-thick rounds
- ½ lb. carrots, sliced in ⅛-inch-thick rounds
- Hot cooked rice or egg noodles for serving, optional

First, make the meatballs. In mixing bowl, combine all meatball ingredients except oil. Mix thoroughly and shape into meatballs about 1 inch in diameter. Heat a small amount of oil in large heavy-bottomed skillet over medium-high heat. Brown meatballs on all sides and transfer to a bowl.

Now start preparing the rest of the stew. In stockpot or Dutch oven, heat the tablespoon of oil over medium heat. Add onion, green pepper and garlic and sauté until softened. Stir in tomatoes with their juices, tomato sauce, oregano, cumin and pepper. Heat to a slow simmer. Add zucchini and carrots; cover and simmer for about 15 minutes.

Add browned meatballs to pot; cover and cook for 20 to 30 minutes longer. Serve with white rice or egg noodles.

NOVEMBER VENISON STEW

Serves: 14 to 16 ✳ Prep Time: 25 minutes ✳ Cooking Time: 2 hours

- 1¼ cups flour
- Salt and pepper
- 4 lbs. boneless venison, cut into 1-inch cubes
- ¼ cup olive oil (approx.), divided
- ½ cup diced celery
- 2 medium onions, diced
- ⅔ cup dry red wine
- 3 beef bouillon cubes, dissolved in ¼ cup hot water
- 1 can (8 oz.) tomato sauce
- 2 cups diced potatoes
- ½ teaspoon pepper
- ½ teaspoon salt
- Garlic powder to taste
- Dry mustard to taste
- 1 can (28 oz.) plum tomatoes, undrained

Heat oven to 325°F. Place flour in large plastic food-storage bag; add salt and pepper to taste and shake well to mix. Measure out ¼ cup of the seasoned flour and set aside. Add cubed venison to bag with remaining seasoned flour, about ½ pound at a time, and toss to coat. In large Dutch oven, heat 2 tablespoons of the oil over medium-high heat until it is hot but not smoking. Brown floured venison cubes in small batches, adding additional oil as necessary. Transfer venison to a plate as it is browned. Set aside.

Add celery and onion to Dutch oven and sauté until tender. Add reserved ¼ cup seasoned flour slowly, stirring constantly, and cook for 2 to 3 minutes. Add wine, bouillon mixture, tomato sauce, potatoes, and remaining spices to Dutch oven. With clean hands, add tomatoes to Dutch oven, squeezing gently to break them apart as you add them; also add juices from tomatoes. Stir well to mix all ingredients. Return venison cubes to Dutch oven and mix gently. Cover and bake for 2 hours.

Venison Meatball Stew

Venison Stew with Barley

Venison Stew with Barley

*Serves: 4 * Prep Time: 30 minutes * Cooking Time: 2 hours*

Since this stew is prepared in a skillet, make sure you have one that's large enough—at least 12 inches in diameter. The aroma while this stew is cooking will have you fighting back hungry ones until it's time to eat!

- ½ lb. pearl onions*
- 9 large fresh shiitake mushrooms, stems removed and discarded (½ to ¾ lb. white mushrooms may be substituted)
- 2 cups peeled, cubed butternut squash (1-inch cubes)
- 1 tablespoon canola oil
- 1¼ teaspoons crumbled dried thyme, divided
- 1½ lbs. boneless venison shoulder or rump, cut into 1-inch cubes
- Seasoned pepper (such as McCormick's California Style Blend Garlic Pepper)
- 3 cups beef stock or canned unsalted beef broth
- 1 bay leaf
- 1 large clove garlic, minced
- ¾ cup pearl barley
- Water as needed (approx. ¾ cup)
- Chopped fresh parsley for garnish

Heat large saucepan of water to boiling. Add pearl onions and boil for 2 to 3 minutes to loosen skins. Drain and cool slightly. Cut off root ends. Squeeze onions from stem end; the onions will slip out of their skins. Place onions in large bowl.

Cut mushroom caps into halves (white mushrooms may be halved or left whole, depending on size). Add mushrooms, squash, oil and 1 teaspoon of the thyme to bowl with onions, stirring gently to coat vegetables. Heat large nonstick skillet over high heat. Add vegetables and sauté until browned. Use slotted spoon to return vegetables to bowl; set aside.

Sprinkle venison with seasoned pepper. Brown seasoned venison cubes in small batches and transfer to a plate. When all venison is browned, return it to skillet. Add beef stock, bay leaf, garlic and remaining ¼ teaspoon thyme. Heat to boiling. Reduce heat, cover and simmer for 15 minutes. Stir in barley. Cover and simmer for 45 minutes. Stir vegetables into stew. Cover and simmer until vegetables and barley are tender, about 45 minutes longer; add water as needed during cooking to keep mixture moist. Remove bay leaf. Sprinkle stew with parsley and serve.

*You can use thawed frozen pearl onions in place of fresh if you'd like; it'll save you some time, as you won't need to boil and peel them.

Warwick Venison Stew

*Serves: 10 to 12 * Prep Time: 20 minutes * Marinating Time: 24 hours * Cooking Time: 3½ hours*

- 3 tablespoons coarsely ground coriander seed
- 2 teaspoons pepper
- ½ teaspoon ground allspice
- 6 cloves garlic, minced
- 3 lbs. boneless venison, cut into 2-inch cubes
- 1 small onion, sliced
- 1 bottle (750 ml) dry red wine, divided
- 1 tablespoon olive oil
- 4 oz. thickly sliced bacon, cut into ¼-inch strips
- 3 bunches of scallions, sliced
- 1 can (14½ oz.) beef broth
- ¾ lb. carrots, peeled and cut into 2-inch lengths
- ¾ lb. potatoes, peeled and cut into ½-inch cubes
- 1 medium parsnip, peeled and cut into 1-inch cubes
- 1 bunch cilantro or parsley, minced

In large glass or plastic bowl, stir together coriander, pepper, allspice and garlic. Add venison and onion; toss to mix well. Add enough wine to cover meat, reserving remaining wine. Cover bowl tightly with plastic wrap and refrigerate for a day, stirring occasionally.

Heat oven to 350°F. Drain marinade from venison, reserving marinade. Blot venison gently with paper towels, being careful not to remove spices from meat's surface. In heavy Dutch oven, heat oil over medium-high heat until it is hot but not smoking. Brown venison cubes in small batches and transfer to a plate as it is browned. Set aside.

Reduce heat to medium and cook bacon until done but not crisp. Using slotted spoon, transfer bacon to plate with venison. Discard fat from Dutch oven, but do not wash it out.

Add scallions, broth, venison and bacon, along with reserved marinade, to Dutch oven. Add enough of the reserved wine to barely cover meat. Cover and heat to simmering over medium heat. Place covered pot in oven; reduce oven temperature to 300°F and bake for 2 hours. Add carrots, potatoes and parsnip to Dutch oven. Re-cover and bake about 1½ hours longer, until meat and vegetables are tender. Sprinkle with fresh herbs and serve.

Chili is a popular dish that is as welcomed on a cold winter's night as it is on a summer's Sunday afternoon. With or without beans, chili attracts enough fanatics to have become a cult. There are organizations throughout the country that dedicate themselves entirely to chili, its ingredients and spices. Some of the groups dedicated to the love of chili include the Chili Appreciation Society (CASI), the International Chili Society (ICS), and the International Connoisseurs of Green & Red Chili (ICG&RC). The CASI and ICS hold numerous cook-offs each year, which attract tens of thousands of chili enthusiasts, also known affectionately as Chilicrats or Chiliheads.

If you're a chili aficionado and have not yet made this dish with venison, you're missing out. Although this is a venison cookbook (and certainly all the venison, including deer, elk, moose and caribou work well in these recipes), it would be neglectful of me to leave out the fact that wild-game chili can also include the meat of boar, javelina, wild turkey, rabbit, squirrel and the like. Try them all. For chili only begs to be tampered with.

QUICKIE VENISON CHILI

Serves: 8 ✳ Prep Time: 20 minutes ✳ Cooking Time: 30 minutes

Sometimes being the chief cook of the house in addition to being a hunter gets to be a bit much to handle, and I find myself caught without food to serve for the midday break during deer season. Should you find yourself in a similar fix, here's a quick recipe for chili that'll satisfy the pangs of hungry hunters in less than an hour!

- 1 large onion, chopped
- 1 green bell pepper, chopped
- 3 cloves garlic, minced
- 2 tablespoons canola oil
- 2 lbs. lean ground venison
- 1 can (15 oz.) kidney beans, drained
- 1 can (11 oz.) corn, drained
- 1 can (28 oz.) whole tomatoes, drained, juices reserved
- 3 tablespoons chili powder
- 2 teaspoons cumin
- 2 teaspoons salt
- 1 bay leaf, crumbled
- 1/8 teaspoon cayenne pepper
- Tortilla chips and shredded cheddar cheese for accompaniment, optional

In Dutch oven, sauté onion, green pepper and garlic in oil over medium heat for about 10 minutes. Add venison and cook until meat is no longer pink, stirring to break up. Add kidney beans and corn; reduce heat to medium-low.

In a small saucepan, mix tomatoes, chili powder, cumin, salt, bay leaf and cayenne pepper with 1/2 cup of the reserved juice from canned tomatoes. Heat to boiling, stirring constantly. Pour over venison mixture in the Dutch oven. Cover and simmer for 30 minutes. Serve with tortilla chips and cheddar cheese.

SLOW-COOKER CHILI

Serves: 8 ✳ Prep Time: 20 minutes ✳ Cooking Time: 6 to 8 hours

Serve this easy chili over hot white rice, topped with shredded cheddar cheese, sour cream, chopped onion, and / or chopped fresh tomatoes.

- 1 lb. ground venison
- 7 cloves garlic, minced
- 3 large onions, chopped
- 1 green bell pepper, chopped
- 1 red bell pepper, chopped
- 2 jalapeño peppers, minced
- 1 can (28 oz.) crushed tomatoes, undrained
- 2 cans (15 oz. each) kidney beans, drained
- 1 cup water
- 1 tablespoon red wine vinegar
- 3 tablespoons chili powder
- 1 teaspoon ground cumin
- 1/2 teaspoon crumbled dried oregano, preferably Mexican
- 1/4 teaspoon ground allspice
- 1/4 teaspoon ground coriander

Cook venison in large skillet over medium-high heat until no longer pink, stirring to break up. Add garlic and onions and cook until onions are tender. Transfer venison mixture to slow cooker. Add remaining ingredients and mix well. Cover and cook on LOW setting for 6 to 8 hours.

Kate's Triple "K" Chili

Serves: 8 ✳ Prep Time: 15 minutes ✳ Cooking Time: 2 hours

Two mouthfuls and you may begin to sweat! This chili recipe is for those with cast-iron stomachs, super macho egos, sadists, or any combination of the above. If there's any left over, remember, chili seems to taste even better the next day!

- 2 lbs. ground venison
- 2 medium onions, chopped
- 1 green bell pepper, chopped
- 3 cloves garlic, minced
- 1 can (28 oz.) whole tomatoes, undrained
- 1 can (15 oz.) tomato sauce
- 1½ cups water
- ⅓ cup sliced serrano peppers (or ½ cup pickled jalapeño peppers, rinsed and chopped)
- ¼ cup chili powder
- 1 tablespoon cayenne pepper
- 1 tablespoon cumin
- ½ teaspoon salt
- ½ teaspoon black pepper
- 1 bay leaf
- 1 can (15 oz.) kidney beans, drained
- Corn bread or rolls for accompaniment, optional

In large Dutch oven, cook venison, onion, green pepper and garlic over medium heat until venison is no longer pink and vegetables have softened, stirring occasionally to break up meat. Add tomatoes, tomato sauce, water, serrano peppers, chili powder, cayenne pepper, cumin, salt, black pepper and bay leaf. Heat to boiling, then reduce heat and simmer, uncovered, for about 1½ hours, stirring occasionally. Add kidney beans and simmer for about 30 minutes longer. Remove bay leaf. Serve chili with corn bread or fresh baked rolls. A cool drink would be nice, too!

marinades, rubs, butters & sauces

everal years ago Peter and I dined at a posh Manhattan restaurant whose claim to fame was their specialty steaks, lamb and veal chops. It took weeks to get a reservation.

When we finally ate there, I was surprised to discover that the meats, while tender and of the proper doneness, lacked something. The waiter offered us a bottle of the house-made steak sauce, but unfortunately it totally overpowered the flavor of the meat. That's the lesson in this chapter: marinades, rubs, butters and sauces should complement the meat's flavor, not compete with it. The meat is the main meal, and its flavor should be the taste that tickles the palate.

Since venison doesn't have a lot of fat, a marinade can serve multiple purposes; the oil adds moisture while the herbs and spices enhance the flavor. A marinade also helps tenderize meat, although it doesn't penetrate very deep. While less common to most cooks, rubs have some distinct qualities that set them apart from marinades: they add flavor to meat without adding additional fat and create a nice crust on the meat. They work well on loins, tenderloins and steaks that are cooked with quick, dry heat methods. Seasoned butters and sauces allow each diner to decide how much flavor (and moisture) to add.

If you're unsure how long your meat should marinate, err on the side of caution—the low end of the given time range—to avoid over-flavoring (this goes for rubs too) or over-tenderizing. One gauge is the color of the meat; if it's beginning to turn gray, remove it from the marinade, pat it dry, wrap it in plastic wrap and return it to the refrigerator until you're ready to cook it. (As with all meat, bring it to room temperature before cooking.) The only exception to the less-is-more rule is if you have a piece of venison from an older animal or one that didn't receive optimum field care. Give it more time to absorb the flavors of a rub or marinade—the high end of the given range—to help mask any gamey flavor it may have.

SPICY BEER MARINADE

*Yield: About 1 quart * Prep Time: 5 minutes*

I like to use this with ribs; I marinate them overnight before roasting or grilling.

- 2 bottles (12 oz. each) beer
- 1 cup honey
- 2 tablespoons lemon juice
- 1 tablespoon light brown sugar
- 1 tablespoon dry mustard
- 2 teaspoons pepper
- 2 teaspoons chili powder
- 1 teaspoon ground sage
- 1 teaspoon salt
- 2 cloves garlic, minced

Open the bottles of beer and take one sip from each bottle, just to make sure they're "fresh." Proceed with recipe. Blend all ingredients and refrigerate in nonreactive container.

SIMPLE MARINADE

*Yield: 1 1/4 cups * Prep Time: 5 minutes*

Great for loin cuts, steaks and roasts. Cover and refrigerate 1 to 3 hours.

- 1 cup olive oil
- 3 tablespoons lemon juice
- 1 tablespoon chopped garlic
- 1 tablespoon crushed black peppercorns
- Crumbled dried oregano to taste

Combine all ingredients in nonreactive container.

When mixing the ingredients for a rub, don't overgrind them; the oils from the spices will be left behind in the grinder or mortar instead of getting worked into the meat.

· · · · · · · · · ·

When grilling venison, turn the cuts of meat with tongs or a spatula. Never pierce the venison with a fork, as this will cause the precious juices to ooze out.

Red Wine Marinade

Yield: About 1 1/2 quarts ✳ Prep Time: 10 minutes ✳ Cooking Time: 5 minutes

Perfect for roasts; marinate for 6 to 8 hours.

- 1½ cups red dry wine
- 1¼ cups red wine vinegar
- 1 cup ketchup
- 1 cup water
- ¾ cup canola oil
- ¼ cup lemon juice
- 1 tablespoon Worcestershire sauce
- 1½ teaspoons crumbled dried thyme
- 2 large onions, chopped
- 2 carrots, chopped
- 2 stalks celery, chopped
- 4 cloves garlic, chopped
- 2 bay leaves

Combine all ingredients in nonaluminum stockpot and heat to boiling. Reduce heat and simmer for about 5 minutes. Cool.

Sesame Ginger Marinade

Yield: About 3/4 cup ✳ Prep Time: 5 minutes

I like to marinate steaks, chops and cutlets in this mixture for 4 to 6 hours prior to cooking. This is also an ideal marinade for meat to be stir-fried.

- ¼ cup Asian sesame seasoning oil
- 3 tablespoons low-sodium soy sauce
- 3 tablespoons minced fresh gingerroot
- 1 tablespoon rice vinegar
- 1 teaspoon dark brown sugar
- 5 scallions, chopped
- 5 cloves garlic, minced
- 3 shallots, minced

Combine all ingredients in nonreactive container.

South-of-the-Border BBQ Rub

Yield: About 1 1/4 cups ✳ Prep Time: 5 minutes

I developed this rub the first time I slow-baked venison ribs. Press it into the ribs and refrigerate them overnight.

- ¼ cup dark brown sugar
- ¼ cup whole black peppercorns
- ¼ cup paprika
- 3 tablespoons garlic powder
- 2 tablespoons salt (kosher, if available)
- 1 tablespoon dry mustard
- 2 teaspoons ancho chili powder
- 1 teaspoon ground cumin

Combine all ingredients in a spice mill and process to a coarse powder, or grind coarsely with a mortar and pestle.

Tri-Color Peppercorn Rub

Yield: About 3/4 cup ✳ Prep Time: 5 minutes

My thought on adding flavor to the quality cuts of venison is, less is more! The peppercorns in this simple rub complement the taste of venison nicely. As they cook over high heat, the peppercorns caramelize and sear into the outer layer of the meat, helping to lock in the juices. This rub works well with grilled or seared sirloin steaks and loin medallions. Marinate 6 to 8 hours.

- 3 tablespoons whole black peppercorns
- 3 tablespoons whole white peppercorns
- 3 tablespoons whole pink peppercorns
- 1 tablespoon mustard seed
- 2 teaspoons garlic powder
- 1½ teaspoons kosher salt

Combine all ingredients in a spice mill and process to a coarse powder, or grind coarsely with a mortar and pestle.

Wasabi Rub

Yield: 1 cup ✳ Prep Time: 20 minutes

Marinate venison steaks with this mixture for 6 to 8 hours.

- 1 tablespoon whole black peppercorns
- 1 tablespoon whole white peppercorns
- 1 tablespoon mustard seed
- 1½ teaspoons wasabi powder (Japanese horseradish)
- 1 tablespoon warm water
- ¼ cup sake (rice wine)
- ¼ cup low-sodium soy sauce
- ¼ cup mirin (sweet Japanese rice wine used for cooking)

Combine peppercorns and mustard seed in a spice mill and process to a coarse powder, or grind coarsely with a mortar and pestle. Set aside.

Place wasabi in small bowl and stir in warm water, a little at a time, until texture is smooth and creamy. Let stand for about 15 minutes at room temperature.

Combine peppercorn mixture with wasabi and remaining ingredients; mix well with a spoon.

GARLIC BUTTER

Yield: 1/2 cup ✳ Prep Time: 15 minutes, plus chilling and forming time

Serve with chops, steaks or burgers.

- 8 cloves garlic
- 1/2 cup unsalted butter (1 stick), softened
- 1/4 teaspoon salt
- Dash white pepper

Place garlic in small saucepan and add water to cover by 1 inch. Heat to boiling; boil for 5 minutes. Drain and set aside to cool slightly.

Cream butter with mixer or food processor. Transfer to small bowl. Press cooled garlic through garlic press into bowl. Add salt and pepper, and stir well. Cover and chill until workable consistency before final forming. For final presentation, shape butter into stick form, or press into individual or larger butter mold(s). It can also be placed in a pastry bag and formed into individual pats; chill formed butter for later service.

HERBED BUTTER

Yield: 1/2 cup ✳ Prep Time: 5 minutes

Delicious with grilled or pan-fried venison steaks.

- 1/2 cup unsalted butter (1 stick), softened
- 1 tablespoon lemon juice
- 1 tablespoon minced fresh flat-leaf parsley
- 1/8 teaspoon ground sage
- Salt and pepper to taste

Cream butter with mixer or food processor, then beat in lemon juice a little at a time. Add the remaining ingredients and mix well. Keep cool until ready to serve.

PEPPERED BUTTER

Yield: 1/2 cup ✳ Prep Time: 5 minutes

This goes well with burgers, chops and steaks.

- 1/2 cup unsalted butter (1 stick), softened
- 1 teaspoon cayenne pepper
- 1/2 teaspoon salt

Cream butter with mixer or food processor, then add spices and cream again. Keep cool until ready to serve.

TOMATO BUTTER

Yield: about 1 cup ✳ Prep Time: 10 minutes

Delicious with grilled or pan-fried venison steaks.

- 1/2 lb. unsalted butter (2 sticks), softened
- 2 or 3 plum tomatoes, blanched, peeled, seeded and minced
- 1/4 teaspoon crumbled dried basil
- Salt and white pepper to taste

Cream butter with mixer, then add remaining ingredients and cream again. Place on wax paper or plastic wrap and roll into log shape about an inch in diameter. Chill thoroughly. Slice round pats of butter to place on grilled burgers or steaks.

CHIMAYO CHILE SAUCE

Yield: 3 cups ✳ Prep Time: 30 minutes

This sauce is based on the fresh chile pepper known as the chimayo, or the New Mexico chile. It is a large, long chile pepper that matures to a deep red color; this is the form that is typically sold fresh. You'll also find this chile dried and strung in garlands, called ristras. The chimayo is grown in the region north of Santa Fe, and whenever we travel to northern New Mexico, I stop into a local market to stock up on these fresh peppers. If you can't find chimayo chiles, you can prepare this sauce with any chile pepper you enjoy. Use it with steaks, roasts, ribs or kabobs.

- 5 large onions, minced
- ½ cup canola oil
- 10 cloves garlic, minced
- 6 oz. chimayo chiles, seeded and chopped
- 1½ cups tomato sauce
- 1 teaspoon sugar

In heavy-bottomed medium saucepan, cook onions in oil over medium heat until soft; do not brown. Add garlic and cook for about 2 minutes. Add chiles and cook for 10 minutes longer. Remove from heat and allow to cool slightly.

Place cooled mixture in food processor. Add tomato sauce and sugar, and process until smooth. Return sauce to saucepan and simmer for 10 minutes. Cool slightly before serving. The sauce can be prepared ahead of time; store in refrigerator and reheat before serving.

Horseradish Cream Sauce

Yield: 1 cup ∗ Prep Time: 10 minutes ∗ Chilling Time: 1 hour or longer

This makes a great dipping sauce for fondue, and also works well as a side for roasts or steaks.

- 1 cup heavy cream
- 2 scallions, minced
- 2 tablespoons fresh grated horseradish
- ¼ teaspoon paprika
- ⅛ teaspoon salt

In large bowl, whip cream until soft peaks form. Stir in scallions, horseradish, paprika and salt. Transfer to glass bowl and chill for 1 hour or longer to allow flavors to blend before serving.

Hunter's Sauce

Yield: 2 cups ∗ Prep Time: 35 minutes

This classic sauce is delicious with venison roasts and pan-fried steaks.

- 3 tablespoons butter
- 1½ teaspoons vegetable oil
- 10 oz. fresh mushrooms, cut into quarters
- 3 shallots, minced
- 2 tablespoons all-purpose flour
- 1 tablespoon finely chopped scallion
- 2 tablespoons brandy
- Salt and pepper
- ½ cup dry white wine
- 1 cup brown sauce or canned beef gravy
- 2 tablespoons tomato sauce
- 1 teaspoon finely chopped fresh parsley

In small saucepan, melt butter in oil over medium heat. Add mushrooms and shallots and sauté until golden brown. Stir in the flour to absorb the juices. Add scallion, brandy, and salt and pepper to taste. Cook over low heat for 2 minutes. Add wine and simmer until liquid is reduced by half. Add brown sauce, tomato sauce and parsley. Heat until sauce starts to bubble, stirring occasionally. Pour into serving dish and serve hot.

Mustard Sauce

Yield: 1 cup ∗ Prep Time: 5 minutes

I serve this as a dipping sauce with fondues. It can also be served as an accompaniment for grilled venison steaks.

- ⅔ cup sour cream or yogurt
- 3 tablespoons mayonnaise
- 1 tablespoon Dijon mustard
- Salt and white pepper to taste

In small bowl, combine all ingredients. Stir well and serve.

BÉCHAMEL SAUCE

*Yield: 3 cups * Prep time: 35 minutes*

*B*échamel is a simple white sauce with a very mild flavor. It is used as a base for many other sauces: cheddar cheese sauce, cream sauce, mornay sauce, mustard sauce and sauce nantua. A classic béchamel is a complicated process. First, veal, herbs and spices are simmered to produce a stock, which is then reduced by half before being enriched with butter. This is rarely done today; the following recipe is much easier, and produces a smooth, creamy sauce.

- ⅓ cup unsalted butter
- ⅓ cup all-purpose flour
- 3 cups milk
- 1 small onion, peeled and halved
- 1 small bay leaf
- Nutmeg and salt

Make the roux: Melt butter in small saucepan over low heat. Slowly sprinkle in the flour, stirring constantly with a wooden spoon. Cook, stirring constantly, until mixture has thickened slightly and is smooth and glossy. Let roux cool slightly.

In another small saucepan, heat milk to scalding over medium-low heat. Add to saucepan with the roux in a thin stream, whisking constantly to prevent lumps. When all milk is thoroughly combined, heat to boiling, stirring constantly. Reduce heat to simmer. Add onion and bay leaf and let simmer for 25 minutes, stirring frequently. During the last 10 minutes, season lightly with nutmeg and salt to taste. The seasonings should not overpower the sauce.

Ideally, the sauce should then be strained through a fine sieve lined with cheesecloth. However, if you don't have these cooking utensils in your kitchen, you may strain the sauce through a wire-mesh strainer to get rid of any major lumps; or, if your sauce is quite smooth, simply remove the onion and bay leaf before serving or using in recipes.

GARLIC SAUCE

*Yield: 1 ½ cups * Prep Time: 10 minutes*

I like to use this as a dipping sauce for fondue, as well as a side sauce for roasts and steaks.

- 2 cups white bread crumbs
- 4 cloves garlic, chopped
- ½ teaspoon salt
- ¼ teaspoon white pepper
- 1 cup olive oil
- 1 tablespoon lemon juice
- 1 tablespoon white wine vinegar

Moisten bread crumbs with a little water. In food processor, combine bread crumbs, garlic, salt and pepper; process until smooth. With the machine running, add olive oil in a thin stream and process until smooth and well blended. Add lemon juice and vinegar, and process until the sauce is creamy. The sauce is now ready for serving.

SPICY FAR EAST DIPPING SAUCE

*Yield: 1 cup * Prep Time: 5 minutes*

This is a delicious dipping sauce for fondue.

- ¼ cup soy sauce
- ¼ cup sesame oil
- 2 tablespoons sake
- 2 tablespoons lemon juice
- 1 tablespoon sesame seeds
- 2 scallions, chopped
- 2 cloves garlic, crushed

Mix all ingredients in small glass bowl. Serve.

game accompaniments

As a lifelong lover and reader of cookbooks, I am always trying the latest recipes, experimenting with new ingredients or tweaking old recipes. Sometimes, when I'm trying to come up with a side dish for a new recipe, nothing hits me right away. That's why I like those cookbooks that include a section on side dishes. I often think, "Well, if this is one of the author's favorites, it should be good enough for me!"

So, here are some of my favorite side dishes to serve with venison. Some, such as the Wild Rice Casserole or the Broccoli Casserole, can be placed in the oven alongside a roast; others, such as the Brown Rice Salad or Corn Relish, can be made in the morning to be served at lunch or dinner time.

Super Herbed Italian Bread (p. 91)

FUSILLI SALAD

Serves: 6 * Prep Time: 15 minutes * Cooking Time: 15 minutes

- 1 tablespoon plus 1½ teaspoons salt
- 1 lb. fusilli pasta
- 1½ lbs. plum tomatoes, seeded and chopped
- 1 small red onion, minced
- 3 fresh basil leaves, chopped
- 2 cloves garlic, minced
- 12 black olives, sliced
- 1 cup julienned romaine lettuce
- ½ cup olive oil
- Salt and freshly ground pepper
- 2 tablespoons grated Parmesan cheese

In stockpot or Dutch oven, combine salt and 4 quarts cold water. Heat to boiling over high heat. Add pasta and cook until al dente according to package directions; stir frequently to prevent sticking.

While pasta is cooking, combine tomatoes, onion, basil, garlic, olives, lettuce and olive oil. Toss to coat well. Season to taste with salt and pepper.

When pasta is al dente, drain in colander and rinse with cold water; drain well. Combine with vegetable mixture and toss to mix thoroughly. Garnish with Parmesan cheese and serve immediately.

BROCCOLI CASSEROLE

Serves: 6 * Prep Time: 10 minutes * Cooking Time: 55 minutes

I usually serve this side dish with roasts, since it can cook in the same oven as most roast recipes.

- 3 eggs
- 1½ cups light cream
- ½ teaspoon dry mustard
- ½ teaspoon salt
- ¼ teaspoon pepper
- 2 cups chopped cooked broccoli
- 1 cup shredded cheddar cheese

Heat oven to 350°F. Lightly grease medium casserole or glass baking dish; set aside. In medium bowl, lightly beat eggs. Add cream, mustard, salt and pepper; mix well. Add broccoli and cheese; stir to combine. Pour broccoli mixture into prepared baking dish. Place baking dish into a larger baking pan. Pour hot water into larger pan to reach halfway up sides of baking dish. Bake for 45 to 55 minutes, or until mixture is set. Serve warm.

Kate's
Grilling Tips

My favorite way to grill corn is to remove some of the outer corn husks and slightly open the inner husks to remove the silk. Then I spread butter (or margarine) on the corn and close the husks around the corn again. I wrap each ear of corn in heavy-duty aluminum foil and twist the ends. Then I place the ears on the grill for about 20 to 30 minutes, turning frequently. I season with salt and pepper once they are cooked and the husks are removed.

• • • • • • • • •

If you love eggplant, try this grilled recipe. Peel eggplant (small ones are more tasty than larger ones) and cut off the ends. Cut into slices about 1 inch thick, but don't cut all the way through the bottom (as you might slice a loaf of garlic bread). Between the slices, add a little butter, salt, pepper, oregano and thin slices of mozzarella cheese and tomato. Wrap tightly in foil. Grill for about 20 minutes, turning every 5 to 7 minutes.

PUNGENT CARAMELIZED ONIONS

Serves: 12 ❋ Prep Time: 5 minutes ❋ Cooking Time: 2½ hours

These go well with steaks, medallions and roasts.

• ¼ cup plus 1 tablespoon olive oil, divided
• 7 large onions (about ½ lb. each)
• ½ teaspoon salt
• 2 tablespoons red wine vinegar

Heat oven to 325°F. Brush 1 teaspoon of the oil on shallow-sided baking sheet. Slice onions into quarters, leaving skin on. Place onions, skin-side down, on prepared baking sheet. Brush with one-quarter of the remaining oil, and sprinkle with the salt. Cover baking sheet with foil and bake for 30 minutes.

Uncover; brush onions with one-third of the remaining oil, and sprinkle with the vinegar. Turn onions so the cut side is down. Bake for 1 hour longer. Brush with half of the remaining oil and turn onions again. Bake for 1 hour longer; brush with remaining oil before serving.

CHEESY GARLIC MASHED POTATOES

Serves: 6 to 8 ❋ Prep Time: 15 minutes ❋ Cooking Time: 25 minutes

• 1 head garlic
• 3 lbs. baking potatoes, peeled and quartered
• 1½ teaspoons salt, divided
• ½ cup unsalted butter (1 stick), melted
• 1 cup shredded cheddar cheese
• ½ cup heavy cream, room temperature
• 1 teaspoon white pepper*

Separate and peel the garlic cloves, then crush them gently with the side of a large, heavy knife. In large saucepan or Dutch oven, combine potatoes, garlic, and 1 teaspoon of the salt. Add water to cover. Heat to boiling over high heat; reduce heat and simmer until potatoes are tender, about 20 minutes. Drain in colander. Press potatoes and garlic through ricer or food mill.

Place hot potatoes in large bowl and beat in butter and cheddar cheese. Gradually mix in cream, pepper and remaining ½ teaspoon salt. Serve hot.

*You don't have to use white pepper. I use it to make the dish look nicer. Black pepper will work just as well.

CORN RELISH

❧

Serves: 6 ✳ Prep Time: 10 minutes ✳ Chilling Time: 2 hours

I like to serve this as a side dish with burgers during the late summer when corn is at its peak!

- 3 tablespoons white wine vinegar
- 2 tablespoons sugar
- 1 teaspoon salt
- ½ cup canola oil
- 1½ cups cooked whole-kernel corn, prepared from fresh or frozen
- ½ cup sliced celery
- ¼ cup pickle relish, drained
- ¼ cup diced red bell pepper
- ¼ cup chopped scallions

In small jar with lid, combine vinegar, sugar and salt. Cover and shake until salt and sugar dissolve. Add oil; re-cover and shake well to blend.

In medium bowl, combine corn, celery, pickle relish, pepper and scallions. Mix well. Pour dressing over the top and mix again. Cover and refrigerate mixture for at least 2 hours. This relish can be made a day ahead.

Kate's Cooking Tips

When preparing a large meal with many side dishes, get your serving dishes out ahead of time and label them accordingly. I write "potatoes," "gravy," "mushrooms," "venison roast," etc., on small pieces of paper and place them into each dish. This way, all my serving dishes are out and ready when the time comes to plate. There is no confusion (amidst entertaining your guests) as to what goes where when it's hot and ready to be served.

• • • • • • • • •

Remember to taste your dish just before serving. This is the last time you can adjust the seasoning.

BROWN RICE SALAD

*Serves: 6 * Prep Time: 10 minutes * Cooking Time: 1 hour*
Chilling Time: 1 hour

- 1 cup brown rice
- 2¼ cups water
- 1 teaspoon butter
- ¼ cup canola oil
- ¼ cup red wine vinegar
- 1 teaspoon balsamic vinegar
- 1 teaspoon salt
- ¾ teaspoon sugar
- ½ teaspoon dried dill weed
- 1 cup cooked whole-kernel corn, prepared from frozen
- 1 cup cooked peas, prepared from fresh or frozen

Combine rice, water and butter in medium saucepan. Heat to boiling; stir once and cover. Reduce heat and simmer for 45 minutes. Remove from heat and let stand, covered, for 5 to 10 minutes. Fluff with fork and transfer to large bowl. Let stand until cool.

In small bowl, combine oil, vinegars, salt, sugar and dill. Mix well. When rice has cooled, add corn and peas to rice and toss to mix well. Pour dressing over mixture and toss to mix well. Cover and refrigerate mixture for at least 1 hour. This salad can be made a day ahead.

RUMMIED SWEET POTATO CASSEROLE

*Serves: 4 * Prep Time: 15 minutes * Cooking Time: 40 minutes*

- 1½ cups thinly sliced apples
- 4 cooked medium sweet potatoes, thinly sliced
- ½ cup light brown sugar
- Cinnamon and allspice to taste
- ¼ cup butter, cut up
- ¼ cup light rum
- ¼ cup water

Heat oven to 350°F. Heat medium saucepan of water to boiling. Add apple slices and cook for about 2 minutes. Drain and rinse with cold water. Lightly grease medium casserole or glass baking dish. Fill dish with alternating layers of potatoes and apples, sprinkling each layer with brown sugar, cinnamon and allspice. Dot top with butter. Mix rum and water and pour over the top. Cover casserole with foil and bake for 40 minutes. Serve warm.

WILD RICE CASSEROLE

*Serves: 6 * Prep Time: 10 minutes * Cooking Time: 2 hours*

- ¾ cup uncooked wild rice
- ¼ cup uncooked brown rice
- 2 stalks celery, chopped
- ¼ cup chopped onion
- 1 quart chicken broth
- ½ cup white wine
- 2 tablespoons butter
- Salt and pepper

Heat oven to 350°F. In medium bowl, mix together the rices, celery, and onion. Transfer to casserole. Add chicken broth, wine, butter, and salt and pepper to taste; stir gently to combine. Cover and bake for 2 hours.

ROASTED HERBED NEW POTATOES

Serves: 8 ✳ Prep Time: 10 minutes ✳ Cooking Time: 1 hour

- 2 lbs. small new potatoes
  (red bliss, fingerling, banana)
- 2 onions, cut into chunks
- ⅓ cup olive oil
- ¼ cup butter, melted
- ¼ teaspoon crumbled dried thyme
- ¼ teaspoon crumbled dried
  rosemary
- ¼ teaspoon crumbled dried
  marjoram
- ½ teaspoon salt
- ¼ teaspoon pepper

Heat oven to 425°F. Combine all ingredients except salt and pepper in medium mixing bowl. Toss to coat. Transfer to large roasting pan and bake until potatoes are done, about 1 hour, turning potatoes every 15 minutes with wooden spoon. Season with salt and pepper before serving.

Summertime Vegetable Pie

SUMMERTIME VEGETABLE PIE

Serves: 6 ✳ Prep Time: 25 minutes ✳ Cooking Time: 45 minutes

When vegetables are fresh from the garden, this dish is at its most piquant. My grandmother used to prepare this, and I now serve it with venison burgers, grilled steaks or shish kabobs.

- 1 medium eggplant, peeled and cubed*
- 2 medium zucchini, cubed*
- 1 large onion, chopped
- ¼ cup canola oil
- 4 medium tomatoes, peeled, cored and chopped
- 3 large eggs
- 1 cup grated Parmesan cheese, divided
- 1 tablespoon minced fresh parsley
- ½ teaspoon crumbled dried basil
- ½ teaspoon crumbled dried oregano
- Salt and pepper
- ⅓ lb. shredded mozzarella cheese (about 1⅓ cups)

Heat oven to 350°F. Lightly grease a pie plate or baking dish; set aside. In large skillet, sauté eggplant, zucchini and onion in oil over medium heat until vegetables are soft. Add tomatoes; cover and simmer for about 15 minutes. Transfer to large bowl; set aside to cool.

In medium bowl, combine eggs, ⅓ cup of the Parmesan cheese, the parsley, basil and oregano. Beat with fork until well blended. Add to vegetables, along with salt and pepper to taste; stir to combine. Pour half of mixture into prepared pie plate. Top with half of the remaining Parmesan cheese. Top with remaining vegetables and Parmesan cheese. Sprinkle the top evenly with the mozzarella cheese. Bake for 40 to 45 minutes, or until mixture is set.

*For a pretty presentation, eggplant and zucchini can be sliced length-wise into thin ribbons, as shown in photo.

SUPER HERBED ITALIAN BREAD

Serves: 8 to 10 ✳ Prep Time: 10 minutes ✳ Cooking Time: 10 minutes

Having grown up in a non-Italian household, I often ate garlic bread that was dressed to the hilt. Mom used all sorts of toppings: garlic, Parmesan or mozzarella cheese, oregano, paprika, butter, and even mayonnaise. Later, when I came to know Peter's Italian family, I realized that while bread was included with the pasta in a true Italian meal, it was usually served hot and plain, or with butter on the side. As a lover of all types of bread, I found this acceptable, but not quite as desirable as what I grew up with. So, here's a recipe for Italian bread with the works. This goes well with Venison Bolognese, charbroiled steaks or chops.

- ½ cup butter (1 stick), preferably room temperature
- 4 cloves garlic, minced
- ½ cup mayonnaise
- ½ cup grated Parmesan cheese
- 1 loaf Italian bread, split lengthwise
- ½ teaspoon crumbled dried oregano
- ½ teaspoon paprika

Set oven to broil and/or 550°F. Melt butter in small saucepan over medium heat. Add minced garlic and cook for about 5 minutes (longer won't hurt); do not let the garlic brown. While that is cooking, combine mayonnaise and Parmesan cheese in small bowl; mix well and set aside.

Place halved Italian bread on baking sheet, crust side down. Drizzle garlic butter over bread. Place bread under broiler and let it brown slightly. Remove from broiler. With spatula, spread mayonnaise mixture on bread. Sprinkle oregano and paprika over mayonnaise mixture. Return bread to broiler and cook until edges are nicely browned. To serve, slice bread into 2-inch-wide strips.

Premier Wild Chefs

Over the eighteen years that I have been co-host of the *Woods N' Water Outdoorsman's Edge* television series, I have been fortunate enough to travel throughout North America to hunt a variety of big game. Not only have I been able to enjoy some of the most exhilarating hunting opportunities a hunter could hope for, but I have been exposed to an added bonus as well: the home-cooked wild-game dishes of each outfitter I hunted with.

Some of these memorable meals were prepared by seasoned wild-game chefs in unique, five-star lodges, and some equally as unforgettable were prepared by camp chefs in cook tents located hours by horseback from civilization. Whether in a commercial kitchen or with the barest of essentials, each chef showed the same inspiration in preparing wild-game meals for their guests.

The meals I enjoyed on these hunts have proved, to me, to be as important as the hunt itself, and they solidified in my mind that for most hunters, preparing and eating wild game is as much a tradition as the hunt itself. Wild game cooking is—in the end—the element that binds the hunt and the eating of game together. Both would be less without the other. Following are some of my favorite outfitter recipes.

Any sportsman who can kill his deer without the tingling spine, the quick clutch at his heart, the delicious trembling of nerve fibers when the game is finally down, has no place in the deer woods.

Lawrence R. Koller, *Shots at Whitetails* (1948)

ANTICOSTI OUTFITTERS BRAISED DEER

Serves: 12 to 15 ✳ Prep Time: 15 minutes ✳ Cooking Time: 2 3/4 hours

The recipe for this delicious braise was graciously provided by the chef at Anticosti Outfitters, and reflects the fine culinary tradition of this lodge.

- 5-lb. venison roast
- ¼ cup butter
- 2 carrots, chopped
- 1 large onion, chopped
- Salt, pepper and garlic powder
- 1 can (14½ oz.) beef broth
- ⅓ cup red wine
- 2 tablespoons all-purpose flour

Heat oven to 325°F. Pat roast dry. In Dutch oven, melt butter over medium-high heat. When it stops sizzling, add roast and brown well on all sides. Transfer roast to plate; set aside.

Add carrots and onion to Dutch oven and cook for 3 to 4 minutes. Season roast with salt, pepper and garlic powder to taste, and return to Dutch oven. Add broth. Cover and bake for 1½ hours.

Add wine and bake for about 1 hour longer, or until roast is cooked to your liking. Transfer roast to serving plate; tent with foil and set aside for 10 to 15 minutes. Meanwhile, sprinkle flour into juices in Dutch oven, whisking constantly; cook over medium heat until thickened. Serve gravy with roast.

Jean-Marie Chretien, General Manager
Safari Anticosti

SAFARI ANTICOSTI OUTFITTERS

Emerging from the prehistoric Champlain Sea, the 3,200-square-mile Anticosti Island spreads across the entry to the majestic Gulf of St. Lawrence. In 1895 the French chocolate magnate Henri Menier bought Anticosti Island for $125,000. He went on to invest another 5 million dollars to turn his island into a paradise. In 1974 it was sold to the Quebec Government for 26 million dollars. In 1984 Anticosti Outfitters Inc., which is owned by Jean Gagnon, obtained an exclusive lease of 400 square miles on the southeastern sector of the island from the government. This area has an estimated population of 15,000 white-tailed deer! The rest is history. Safari Anticosti Outfitters has developed the most prestigious deer-hunting grounds in the province of Quebec, investing over 12 million dollars along the way to accomplish its goal.

I was first invited to hunt at Safari Anticosti Outfitters in 1990. Besides getting my two whitetails, I also had the rare opportunity to see seals, whales and uncountable numbers of birds in a variety of colors. The accommodations were top-shelf, but what really impressed me was the food. After each day's hunt, the guests would gather at the log lodge, which was perched on the edge of a sandy cliff overlooking the Atlantic Ocean and mouth of the St. Lawrence Seaway. There, with white-linen table service, we dined on five-course French gourmet cuisine including smoked salmon and oyster appetizers, fine French wine, melon soup, prime rib and mouthwatering homemade desserts. Peter has hunted with Anticosti Outfitters several times since and assures me that with each passing year the hunting, service and food only get better.

(418) 786-5788 ✳ *www.safarianticosti.com*

Sun Canyon Ranch Crock-Pot Pepper Steak

Serves: 6 to 8 ✳ Prep Time: 15 minutes ✳ Cooking Time: 10 to 11 hours

For a great meal, serve this stew over grilled polenta slices or corn bread.

- 2 lbs. venison steak (deer or elk)
- ½ cup all-purpose flour
- 2 tablespoons canola oil (approx.)
- 1 can (14½ oz.) tomatoes, undrained
- 2 green bell peppers, sliced
- 1 large onion, sliced
- 6 oz. fresh mushrooms, sliced
- 3 tablespoons soy sauce
- 3 tablespoons molasses
- Salt and pepper

Cut steak into strips and dredge with flour. In medium skillet, heat oil over medium-high heat until hot but not smoking. Brown venison strips in small batches, transferring to slow cooker as they are browned.

In small bowl, combine tomatoes, peppers, onion, mushrooms, soy sauce, molasses, and salt and pepper to taste. Mix well. Pour mixture over venison. Cover and cook on HIGH for 1 hour, then reduce heat to LOW and cook for 9 to 10 hours longer.

Susan and Lee Carlbom
Sun Canyon Lodge, Augusta, MT

Sun Canyon Ranch

I first met Lee and Susan Carlbom in 1987. Their outfit is uniquely western, invoking a true feeling of wilderness hunting. Located in the eastern gateway to the Lewis and Clark Forest and the unique Bob Marshall Wilderness Area, Sun Canyon Ranch provides excellent hunting opportunities for both mule deer and elk. It also gives clients a chance to revitalize their spirit as they venture into the last of the true mountain wilderness areas of the continental United States. What struck me most about this facility is that no matter where we were, either at the lodge or in the wilderness, Lee and Susan somehow managed to prepare delicious meals indigenous to the West.

1-888-749-3654 ✳ www.suncanyonlodge.com

LUCKY STAR RANCH VENISON STEW

Serves: 6 ✳ Prep Time: 20 minutes ✳ Cooking Time: 2 hours

We serve this stew with sour cream, baguettes and a nice fresh green salad. It is an ideal menu for a large crowd, because the stew can be prepared beforehand and gently reheated just before serving.

- 2 lbs. venison stew cubes
- 1½ cups all-purpose flour
- 1 tablespoon butter
- 1 tablespoon oil
- Salt, pepper, paprika and chili powder
- 4 onions, cut into quarters
- 1 or 2 cans (14½ oz. each) tomatoes, undrained
- 1 cup heavy cream, or a little more as needed
- ½ cup ketchup
- ½ cup red wine, or a little more as needed
- 1 package (2.4 oz.) Knorr goulash mix, optional
- Tomato juice, optional

Pat venison cubes dry; dust with flour. In large skillet, melt butter in oil over medium-high heat. Brown venison cubes in small batches, transferring to Dutch oven or stockpot as it is browned. Season browned venison with salt, pepper, paprika and chili powder to taste. Add onions, tomatoes, cream, ketchup and wine, and goulash mix if using. Cover Dutch oven. Simmer for 2 hours, stirring every 30 minutes; make sure stew meat is always covered with liquid, adding more cream (at room temperature), wine or tomato juice, depending upon your taste.

Baron Josef von Kerckerinck
Lucky Star Ranch, Chaumont, NY

LUCKY STAR RANCH

As the founder of the North American Deer Farmer's Association, Baron Josef von Kerckerinck knows a lot about deer. On his stately 5,000-acre Lucky Star Ranch in upstate New York, Josef has raised and managed all types of game—European red stag, fallow deer and a host of other non-native deer. Over the last several years, he has been steadily converting the ranch to a strictly white-tailed deer hunting ranch. A native of Germany, Josef brings the European aspect to all his client's hunts with true European shooting houses for the hunt and, most importantly, European-style meals for the guests.

There are few that can come close to Josef's hospitality at his multi-faceted facility. He has always made my family and me feel more than welcome whenever we visit. Over the years, Peter and I have enjoyed great deer hunting at the Lucky Star, and it was here that my son Cody, at the age of nine, shot his first deer—a memory we'll cherish forever.

(315) 649-5519 ✳ www.luckystarranch.com

TUCKAMORE LODGE SALISBURY MOOSE STEAK WITH MUSHROOM SAUCE

Serves: 4 ✳ Prep Time: 15 minutes ✳ Cooking Time: 15 minutes

With this recipe, Peggy Mitchelmore turns what seems like just another Salisbury steak recipe into something quite memorable. Serve this with baked potatoes and green beans or steamed broccoli.

Patties:
- 1 lb. ground moose
- ¾ cup cracker crumbs
- 1 tablespoon Worcestershire sauce
- ½ teaspoon onion powder
- ½ teaspoon steak spice
- ½ teaspoon salt
- ¼ teaspoon pepper
- ¼ teaspoon garlic powder

Sauce:
- 2 tablespoons butter
- 1 can (8 oz.) mushrooms, drained and chopped
- 2 tablespoons all-purpose flour
- 1 teaspoon curry powder
- 1 cup hot water
- 1 beef bouillon cube

In a bowl, combine all patty ingredients. Mix gently but thoroughly. Divide evenly and shape into 4 patties.

In small saucepan, melt butter over medium heat. Add mushrooms and sauté for 2 to 3 minutes. Blend in flour and curry powder. Add hot water and bouillon cube. Cook, stirring constantly, until smooth and thickened.

While sauce is thickening, either pan-fry or grill the patties for 2 to 3 minutes per side. Pour sauce over each patty and serve.

Peggy Mitchelmore
Tuckamore Lodge
Main Brook, Newfoundland

TUCKAMORE LODGE

Barb Genge is the president and owner of Tuckamore Lodge, a first-class operation with Scandinavian-style accommodations in the heart of rugged Newfoundland wilderness. Whether you are there to whale-watch, observe towering icebergs, visit the ancient Viking settlements, or, as we were, to hunt moose, you will experience Tuckamore's hospitality and professionalism. This facility is world renowned in adventure tourism and is recognized as one of the six best lodges in all of Canada. Guests are treated to three sit-down meals a day in the luxurious comfort of the main log cabin lodge. Prepared by a culinary staff headed by Peggy Mitchelmore, each meal, especially dinner, is exquisitely prepared and scrumptious. During our stay, we dined on meals fit for a king, as well as a wide array of fabulous desserts like Death by Chocolate and Gooseberry Pie. Peter and I hunted moose with Barb on two occasions and came home with enough moose meat to try many of the moose recipes the staff so generously shared with us.

1-888-865-6361 ✳ www.tuckamore-lodge.nf.net

Conklin's Lodge Venison Roll-Ups

Serves: 8 to 10 as appetizers, 4 to 6 as main dish ✳ Prep Time: 15 minutes ✳ Cooking Time: 10 minutes

- 2 lbs. boneless venison steaks
- Garlic powder, salt and pepper
- 1 lb. sliced bacon

Slice steaks across the grain into ¼-inch-thick strips. Arrange strips in a single layer on work surface. Sprinkle the tops with garlic powder, salt and pepper to taste. Roll each slice jelly-roll-style with the seasoned side in. Wrap each roll with a portion of bacon, trimming bacon according to the thickness of the roll, and secure with a wooden toothpick. Cook rolls in skillet over medium heat until bacon is cooked, turning to cook evenly. Remove toothpicks before serving.

Marie Conklin
Conklin's Lodge and Camps, Patten, ME

Conklin's Lodge and Camps

Located in the gorgeous deep woods at the north entrance to Baxter State Park (which boasts nearly 205,000 acres of wilderness), Conklin's Lodge and Camps offers excellent year-round hunting, fishing and outdoor activities. Registered Maine Guide Lester Conklin and his wife, Marie, have been operating their lodge since 1987. In addition to highly successful guided bear and white-tailed deer hunts, guests of Conklin's also enjoy pursuing grouse, woodcock, snowshoe hare or even winter coyotes, with or without a guide. Whether you're with a top-notch guide or you adventure out on your own, you'll feel the true spirit of the deep northern backwoods in this area. While on stand, you may see moose, bobcat, lynx, red fox, marten or even a fisher. When you return to camp, you'll be treated to one of Marie's delicious meals, which include favorites such as glazed baked ham, roast pork with gravy, homemade lasagna and stuffed Cornish hen.

(207) 528-2901 ✳ www.conklinslodge.com

Cedar Ridge Outfitters Red Stroganoff

CEDAR RIDGE OUTFITTERS RED STROGANOFF

Serves: 8 to 10 ✳ Prep Time: 10 minutes ✳ Cooking Time: 3 to 4 hours

Here's one of Debbie Blood's camp favorites. Serve it with a heaping bowl of hot white rice.

- 3 tablespoons vegetable oil (approx.)
- 3 lbs. boneless venison, cut into ¾-inch cubes
- 2 cans (14½ oz. each) whole tomatoes, drained, juices reserved
- 2 cans (14½ oz. each) beef consommé
- 4 cans (8 oz. each) tomato sauce
- 2 cups sliced fresh mushrooms
- 1 large onion, sliced
- 1 green bell pepper, sliced

Heat oven to 350°F. In large skillet, heat 1 tablespoon of the oil over medium-high heat until hot but not smoking. Brown venison cubes in small batches, adding additional oil as necessary. Transfer venison to a Dutch oven as it is browned.

When all venison has been browned, slice drained tomatoes and add to Dutch oven with venison. Add remaining ingredients including reserved tomato juice; stir gently. Cover and bake for 2 hours, then check consistency. If the mixture seems to have too much liquid, remove the lid before continuing; if the mixture seems too thick, stir in a little water and re-cover. If the venison is tender at this point, bake for 1 hour longer; if it is a little tough, bake for 2 hours longer, or until venison is tender.

Debbie and Hal Blood
Cedar Ridge Outfitters, Jackman, ME

CEDAR RIDGE OUTFITTERS

Hal and Debbie Blood own Cedar Ridge Outfitters. They have been successfully guiding deer, moose and bear hunters in the woods around Jackman, Maine for 20 years. Deer hunting at Cedar Ridge is typical of Maine. You don't see a lot of deer every day, nor bucks in a week. But when you do see a buck, more often than not it's a dandy!

Peter and I first met Hal in the mid-'80s, and later got to know his wife, Debbie. She is a licensed and expert Maine guide who also commands the base operation. On our last visit, we thoroughly enjoyed both the Bloods' hospitality and some of the finest home-cooked meals I have had the pleasure of eating. All meals are served family-style, and Debbie always makes sure they're served piping hot and delicious.

(207) 668-4169 ✳ www.cedarridgeoutfitters.com

Legends Ranch Herbed Venison Rolls

❧

Serves: 5 to 8 ✳ Prep Time: 1¼ hours ✳ Cooking Time: 30 minutes

When we visited, the side dishes served with this entrée included basil pesto-stuffed tortellini with tomato sauce, fresh steamed asparagus spears and a fresh garden salad. The recipe below has been halved for home use.

Cheese Filling:

- 8 oz. cream cheese, softened
- 3 large cloves garlic, minced
- 1½ teaspoons Italian herb blend
- ¾ cup shredded mozzarella cheese
- 2 small eggs, beaten
- 1 jalapeño pepper, minced

- 2- to 3-lb. boneless venison sirloin tip or tender rump roast, well trimmed

Breading:

- 3 cups all-purpose flour
- ¼ cup seasoning blend of your choice (if using seasoned salt, use a lower-sodium type)
- 1½ cups Italian-seasoned bread crumbs
- 4 eggs, beaten
- ½ cup milk

- Shortening for deep-frying

Make the cheese filling: In glass bowl, combine cream cheese, garlic and herbs; mix well. Add remaining filling ingredients; mix until creamy. Reserve in refrigerator.

Prepare the venison: Cut roast across the grain into ¾-inch-thick steaks. You should get 5 to 8 steaks, depending upon the size of the roast. Place steaks on lightly oiled work surface (the oil prevents the meat from sticking). Place plastic wrap over steaks to prevent splattering. Gently pound steaks with tenderizing mallet to about ⅛-inch thickness. At this point, each steak should be about 6 inches in diameter.

Place a large spoonful of the chilled cheese filling on a steak, an inch from the edge nearest you; use only as much filling as the steak can hold. Fold the sides of the steak over the filling. Then, roll up the steak jelly-roll-style and place, seam-side down, in a single layer on a sheet pan. When all rolls are complete, place in freezer for about 20 minutes to harden the cheese.

While rolls are in the freezer, combine flour and seasoning in food processor and pulse to mix well; alternately, stir together in large bowl. Place flour mixture in large pan. Place bread crumbs in a separate pan. Mix eggs with milk and place in shallow container.

Heat oven to 275°F. Remove venison rolls from freezer and let stand for about 5 minutes, which will allow the meat to "sweat" prior to being breaded. Coat each venison roll with the flour mixture, then place in egg wash and coat well. Roll in breadcrumbs and set aside.

In deep skillet over high heat, melt enough shortening to cover several rolls; heat shortening to 350°F. Fry rolls, a few at a time, for about 1 minute each. This will seal the meat and turn the crust a light golden brown. Transfer rolls to a jelly-roll pan (large baking sheet with sides) as they are fried. When all have been fried, place pan in oven for 10 to 15 minutes, until rolls are a rich brown.

John Eye
Legends Ranch, Bitely, MI

Legends Ranch

Legends Ranch is owned and operated by Skipper Bettis and Keith Johnson. Between them, they have nearly 75 years of deer-hunting experience. The deer hunting at this ranch is truly legendary. My son, Cody (who was 11 at the time), and I were invited to hunt at Legends Ranch in 2000. We both shot terrific 8-point bucks and saw some real wall hangers during our hunt, too.

Lodging and meals at the Legends Ranch are as outstanding as the hunting. Chef John Eye treats all guests to gourmet meals you would normally find at the finer restaurants across the country. During our stay, Chef Eye and I had many conversations about his experiences as a professional chef, and his love for preparing wild game. During these conversations I decided that one of John's wild-game recipes would be a valued addition to this book.

(800) 972-9092 ✳ www.legendsranch.com

WHALE RIVER LODGE CARIBOU STROGANOFF

Serves: 4 ✳ Prep Time: 10 minutes ✳ Cooking Time: 2 hours

The head chef at Whale River shared many caribou recipes with me, and I have used them to prepare meat from the two trophy-class bulls I took at the camp. The recipe that has received the most acclaim is this delicious caribou stroganoff. Serve over cooked rice or noodles, accompanied by a salad.

- 2 lbs. caribou steak
- 2 tablespoons butter
- 4 cups water
- 1 package (1 oz.) onion soup mix
- 2 tablespoons chopped fresh parsley
- 1½ teaspoons garlic powder
- ¼ teaspoon crumbled dried oregano
- Pepper
- ½ cup sour cream
- ¼ cup cornstarch

Cut steak into 1-inch cubes. In Dutch oven, brown cubes in butter over medium-high heat. Add water, onion soup mix, parsley, garlic powder, oregano, and pepper to taste; stir well. Heat to boiling. Reduce heat to low and cook for about 1½ hours, stirring occasionally. When caribou is tender, remove about 2 tablespoons of the liquid from the Dutch oven and stir into the sour cream, along with the cornstarch; this raises the temperature of the sour cream to prevent curdling. Stir sour cream mixture into liquid in Dutch oven and cook, stirring frequently, until sauce thickens.

Alain Tardif
Whale River Lodge Outfitters, northern Quebec, Canada

WHALE RIVER LODGE

The vast openness of the northern Canadian tundra is both beautiful and stark. Across thousands of miles each year, a distant cousin of the white-tailed deer makes its annual trek. Alain Tardif, owner of Whale River Lodge, has been in the caribou outfitting business for 30 years and has mastered the secret of bringing clients to the areas where the caribou are. On top of that, he has built and staffed lodges that cater to every hunter's needs in areas that are so remote, the only population is native Inuits. I knew we would be traveling far into northern Quebec, but it wasn't until we traveled by jet plane for 2½ hours north of Montreal, then flew by floatplane for another 2 hours, that I realized how far north we were really going! How they get the equipment needed, especially for the kitchen, to these remote places is mind-boggling. But, according to Alain, having the comforts of home is all-important to the hunt, especially when it comes to mealtime.

(800) 463-4868 ✳ www.whaleriverlodge.com

Midwest Venison Casserole

Serves: 6 to 8 ✻ Prep Time: 15 minutes ✻ Cooking Time: 1 1/4 to 1 3/4 hours

The home-cooked meals at Midwest USA are just as memorable as the hunting. I have made this recipe several times for family and guests. Every single guest has asked me for the recipe. So, here it is.

- 2 lbs. ground venison
- One-quarter of a medium onion, diced
- 4 cans (10¾ oz. each) condensed cream of mushroom soup
- 1 bag (24 oz.) frozen vegetable of your choice
- 1 bag (32 oz.) frozen Tater Tots

Heat oven to 375°F. In large skillet, cook venison and onion over medium heat until venison is no longer pink and onion has softened, stirring occasionally to break up meat. Drain any fat. Spread venison on bottom of 9x13x2-inch baking dish. Spread 2 cans of the undiluted soup over venison. Next, distribute frozen vegetables on top. Spread remaining 2 cans of undiluted soup over vegetables. Finally, top with frozen Tater Tots. Cover with foil and bake for 45 minutes. Uncover and bake for 15 to 30 minutes longer. Let sit for about 10 minutes before serving.

Rodney Hughes
Midwest USA Outfitters, Cantril, Iowa

Midwest USA

As most deer hunters know, Iowa is among the top states in the nation for bagging a trophy-class whitetail buck. Rod Hughes owns Midwest USA Outfitters in Cantril, in the southeastern portion of the state. The whitetail hunting here is exciting because a hunter never knows when the next Iowa Boone & Crockett record-book buck will walk into the sights. I always enjoy hunting in Iowa because of this anticipation.

(888) 530-8492 ✻ *http://midwest-usa.hypermart.net*

Your Best Recipes

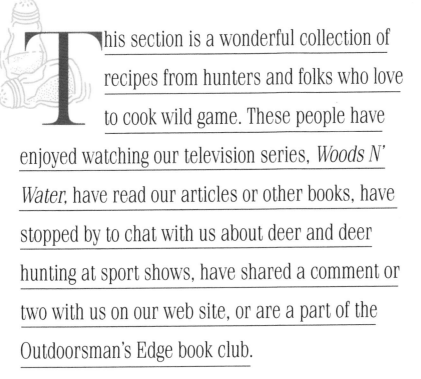

This section is a wonderful collection of recipes from hunters and folks who love to cook wild game. These people have enjoyed watching our television series, *Woods N' Water*, have read our articles or other books, have stopped by to chat with us about deer and deer hunting at sport shows, have shared a comment or two with us on our web site, or are a part of the Outdoorsman's Edge book club.

I have tried all their delicious recipes. Many are simple and quick to cook, while others are a little more elaborate and time-consuming. If I altered the recipe or tried something a little different, you'll see my note at the bottom of the recipe.

The recipe I found to be a favorite among many of my friends and family is Grilled Peppered Venison Loin with Portobello Sauce. My mouth waters just writing about it. I came across this recipe during a wild-game recipe contest we held for the book club members of Outdoorsman's Edge. Although the hundreds of recipes we received were all winners, this one took first place. It's unique because it has to be made over a grill (indoors or out) and includes one of my favorite mushrooms—portobello. It is absolutely delicious. In fact, once I had tested it and selected it as the winner, I decided to make the dish for an upcoming *Woods N' Water* television segment. At the end of the taping session, the camera crew couldn't wait to dig in. Within minutes, the entire dish was consumed. How good was it? After some of the crew members finished their own servings, they started swiping portions from other people's plates. Even when it was gone, they wiped up the remaining sauce with bread! I hope you'll enjoy each of the dishes in this section as much as I do.

BONELESS ROAST WITH CREAMY PEPPERCORN SAUCE

Serves: 5 to 8 ✳ Prep Time: 5 minutes ✳ Marinating Time: 12 hours ✳ Cooking Time: 40 to 60 minutes

Marinade:

- ¼ cup soy sauce or teriyaki sauce
- ¼ cup Gravy Master
- 1 tablespoon Worcestershire sauce
- 3 cloves garlic, minced
- Seasoned salt to taste
- Chopped fresh parsley to taste

- 2- to 3-lb. boneless venison roast

Creamy Peppercorn Sauce:

- 1 pkg. (1 oz.) Knorr peppercorn sauce mix
- ¾ cup water
- ¼ cup heavy cream
- 2 tablespoons cognac
- 2 teaspoons prepared horseradish

In nonreactive bowl, combine all marinade ingredients. Add venison, turning to coat. Cover and refrigerate overnight, turning occasionally.

Heat oven to 350°F. Remove roast from marinade; discard marinade. Place roast on rack in baking pan. Roast, uncovered, to desired doneness (see chart, p. 24), 15 to 25 minutes per pound. Remove roast from oven when internal temperature is 5° less than desired. Let meat rest for 10 to 15 minutes before slicing.

While the roast is resting, make the sauce: In small saucepan, combine all sauce ingredients. Whisk until well blended. Heat to boiling over medium-high heat, stirring constantly. Reduce heat and simmer for 4 to 5 minutes, stirring occasionally. Serve sauce with sliced roast.

Leo Somma, Hampton Bays, NY

"1000-YEAR-OLD" STEW

Serves: 4 to 6 ✳ Prep Time: 15 minutes ✳ Cooking Time: 6½ hours

A student of the Pawnee Indians and collector of old recipes and cookbooks, M. J. Paulk sent in this recipe to share. He writes, "This is an original recipe made with ingredients available to the Paleo Indians of the Upper Republic Culture of about 800 A.D. on the Republican River in southwestern Nebraska. Archaeological findings around Cambridge, Stockville and Curtis, Nebraska verify the ingredients. The people of this era had very little, if any, salt."

- 2 lbs. buffalo, deer or elk stew meat, cut into 1-inch cubes
- 1 cup water
- 1 package (6 oz.) long-grain and wild rice* (do not use the supplied seasoning packet)
- Half of a medium onion, or to taste, unchopped
- ½ teaspoon crumbled dried sage, preferably home grown
- Salt to taste (rare in 800-900 A.D.)
- 1 cup unsalted roasted sunflower nutmeats
- 1 can (15 oz.) yellow or white hominy, drained, rinsed and drained again
- 2 cups cooked pinto beans** (you may substitute navy, great northern, lima or red beans)

Place meat in 3-quart slow cooker. Add water, rice, onion, sage and salt. Cover and cook on HIGH for 3½ hours. Stir in sunflower seeds, hominy and beans. Reduce heat to LOW and cook for 3 hours longer. Add water or broth to thin your stew to desired consistency before serving.

This is a fairly bland stew. Properly salted, I like it as is; however, you may want to add ketchup, steak sauce or chili powder to suit modern tastes. If you don't care for hominy or sunflower seeds, they can be left out. It will still be authentic and tasty. Do not freeze leftovers of this stew, as it gets mushy when frozen.

*If using instant rice mix, add it with the hominy rather than at the beginning.

**If using uncooked beans rather than cooked, put them in with the meat and onions, adding a little more water.

Kate's note: I tried this recipe with venison stew meat, wild rice, cooked beans, hominy and sunflower seeds in the slow cooker. I did have to add water from time to time, but it was surprisingly good, seasoned with a little chili powder. Take a step back in time with this recipe!!

M. J. Paulk (The Mountain Man), Wood River, NE

GRILLED PEPPERED VENISON LOIN WITH PORTOBELLO SAUCE

Serves: 6 ✳ Marinating Time: 2 hours ✳ Prep Time: 30 minutes ✳ Cooking Time: 20 minutes

This recipe from Mark Alexander placed first in the Outdoorsman's Edge recipe contest. It is as delicious as it sounds! Mark says, "I typically serve this with a steamed vegetable and parsleyed red potatoes. This spicy-hot meal will melt in your mouth, and is even better with a frosty beer and a friend! Enjoy."

- 2 cans (12 oz. each) beer
- ½ cup Greek salad dressing
- ¼ cup Worcestershire sauce
- 2 venison tenderloins, about 1 lb. each

Sauce:
- 1½ cups whole milk or cream
- 8 oz. crumbled feta cheese
- 3 tablespoons sour cream
- 8 to 10 portobello mushrooms, finely diced
- 4 to 6 whole green peppercorns, optional
- Dash of cayenne pepper

- ½ cup Caesar salad dressing
- 12 portobello mushroom slices
- ¼ cup white pepper
- ¼ cup black pepper
- 6 cloves garlic

In large bowl, stir together beer, Greek dressing and Worcestershire sauce. Add tenderloins, turning to coat. Cover and refrigerate for 2 hours, turning occasionally. (I like to marinate in a resealable plastic container so that I may shake it now and then.)

When venison has marinated for 2 hours, prepare grill for high heat; light coals or preheat gas grill.

Begin preparing the sauce: In medium saucepan, combine milk, feta cheese and sour cream. Heat to boiling over medium heat, stirring frequently. Reduce heat to low and add diced mushrooms, green peppercorns and cayenne. Allow to simmer, stirring occasionally, while preparing tenderloins.

Place Caesar dressing in a bowl; arrange sliced mushrooms on a plate. Set both aside with a basting brush. Drain and discard marinade from tenderloins; pat dry. Sprinkle tenderloins on both sides with white and black pepper; squeeze garlic over meat with garlic press. Rub seasonings into meat, piercing with a fork as you rub. The fork tenderizes the meat even further, and allows the pepper to penetrate. After 2 or 3 minutes of poking and rubbing, the meat is ready to grill. Remove sauce from heat; set aside and keep warm.

Place tenderloins on grate and grill, brushing periodically with Caesar dressing and turning as needed. When tenderloins are about half cooked, submerge mushroom slices in dressing and place on grill. Rotate mushrooms after about 1 minute to create diamond-shaped grill markings. Grill until tenderloin is desired doneness, brushing tenderloins and mushrooms occasionally with dressing.

Thinly slice tenderloins into ½-inch-thick slices and arrange on serving platter. Pour sauce over the meat and top with the grilled mushrooms.

Kate's note: For medium-rare, grill until the internal temperature is about 125°F. The temperature will increase slightly once the meat has been removed from the grill.

Mark E. Alexander, Mifflinburg, PA

DOWN-HOME JERKY

Yield: 60 to 70 slices ✻ *Prep Time: 10 minutes* ✻ *Marinating Time: 12 hours* ✻ *Cooking/Drying time: 8 to 10 hours*

- 3 lbs. venison rump meat
- ½ cup barbecue sauce
- ¼ cup Worcestershire sauce
- 2 tablespoons lemon juice
- 1 tablespoon spicy brown mustard
- 1 tablespoon lemon pepper
- 1 tablespoon honey
- 1 teaspoon liquid smoke
- 1 teaspoon salt
- ½ teaspoon garlic powder
- ½ teaspoon Old Bay seasoning
- ½ teaspoon freshly ground black pepper

Cut venison into ¼-inch-thick slices. In large nonreactive bowl, combine all remaining ingredients; blend with whisk. Add meat and stir well. Cover and refrigerate overnight, stirring occasionally.

Line bottom of oven with foil to catch drips. Hang venison strips by toothpicks from oven racks. Set oven to 150°F and prop oven door open about 2 inches using a ball of foil or an empty can. Cook-dry venison for 8 to 10 hours.

Dan Moyer, Camphill, PA

"Refrigerator-Smoked" Venison Ham

Serves: 20 to 25 ✳ *Prep Time: 30 minutes* ✳ *Marinating Time: 2 hours to 2 days* ✳ *Cooking Time: 3 hours*

- 1 cup packed brown sugar
- 1 jar (2.75 oz.) imitation bacon-flavored bits
- 1 tablespoon plus 1½ teaspoons pepper
- ½ teaspoon salt
- ½ teaspoon minced garlic
- ½ teaspoon ground sage
- 1 boned venison hindquarter (10 to 13 lbs. after boning)
- 1 bottle (5 oz.) Worcestershire sauce
- Liquid smoke

In medium bowl, combine sugar, bacon bits, pepper, salt, garlic and sage. Mix thoroughly; set aside.

Lay boned hindquarter on work surface with the inside facing up. Make small cuts until the meat will lie flat. Baste thoroughly with Worcestershire sauce. Sprinkle with 5 or 6 shakes of liquid smoke. Sprinkle three-quarters of the sugar mixture evenly over venison; rub seasonings and sugar mixture into meat well.

Tie a slipknot on one end of a 3-foot-long piece of heavy kitchen twine. Roll meat up tightly, then slip the noose around and draw tightly. Wrap the rest of the twine around the meat and tie tightly; an extra pair of hands comes in handy during this step! Baste again with Worcestershire sauce, and sprinkle with 5 or 6 shakes of liquid smoke. Rub remaining sugar mixture all over ham.

Place in large plastic food-storage bag or oven-roasting bag; place in roasting pan to prevent leakage. Refrigerate for at least 2 hours, or as long as 2 days. Bake in oven at 275°F for 3 hours. Serve hot.

James A. Compton, Knoxville, TN

Tangy Venison Stew

Serves: 12 ✳ *Prep Time: 45 minutes* ✳ *Cooking Time: 7 hours*

- ¼ cup olive oil (approx.), divided
- 3 lbs. boneless venison, cut into 1-inch cubes
- 2 onions, preferably Vidalia, chopped
- 1 medium head of garlic, peeled and minced
- 6 cups beef broth
- 1½ cups burgundy or other dry red wine
- 1 can (5½ oz.) spicy-hot V8 juice
- 3 tablespoons Worcestershire sauce
- 6 carrots, sliced
- 2 packages (12 oz. each) fresh mushrooms
- 2 tablespoons chopped fresh parsley
- 2 tablespoons crumbled dried basil
- 1 tablespoon crumbled dried oregano
- 1 teaspoon crumbled dried thyme
- 1 teaspoon cayenne pepper (if possible, use 1 tablespoon Vietnamese "Tuong Ot Toi" garlic chili sauce instead), optional
- 6 red potatoes, skin on, cut into ¾-inch cubes
- 1 can (11 oz.) peas, drained
- Flour or cornstarch to thicken gravy
- Salt and pepper

In large skillet, heat 2 tablespoons of the oil. Brown venison cubes in small batches, adding additional oil as necessary. Transfer venison to a plate as it is browned. Set aside.

In large Dutch oven, sauté onions and garlic in 1 teaspoon of the oil over medium heat until onion is soft. Add broth, wine, juice and Worcestershire sauce. Heat to boiling. Reduce heat and simmer for 5 minutes. Add browned venison, carrots, mushrooms, parsley, basil, oregano, thyme and cayenne. Simmer for about 6 hours, stirring occasionally. Add potatoes and peas. Return to boiling. Reduce heat and simmer until potatoes are tender, about 1 hour longer. Make a thin flour-water slurry and use to thicken gravy as needed just before serving; add salt and pepper to taste.

Kate's note: A delicious recipe in which I substituted frozen peas for the canned (my own preference).

Ernest P. Moore, Gloversville, NY

Venison Bourguignon

Serves: 6 to 8 ✳ Prep Time: 30 minutes ✳ Cooking Time: 1³/4 hours

- 4 slices bacon
- ½ cup all-purpose flour
- 2 teaspoons salt
- ¼ teaspoon pepper
- 3 lbs. venison stew meat, cut into 1-inch cubes
- ½ cup canola oil or corn oil
- ¼ cup minced onion
- 1 teaspoon minced garlic
- ¼ cup brandy
- 1 cup burgundy or other dry red wine
- 1 cup beef broth
- 2 bay leaves
- 1 cup sliced fresh mushrooms
- Hot cooked noodles

In Dutch oven, cook bacon until very crisp. Transfer bacon to paper towel–lined plate, reserving drippings; set bacon aside. Place flour, salt and pepper in large plastic food-storage bag and shake well to mix. Add cubed venison and toss to coat.

Add oil to bacon drippings in Dutch oven; heat over medium-high heat until hot but not smoking. Add onion and garlic, and cook until onion is soft, stirring frequently. Add half of the floured venison cubes and brown well on all sides. Transfer venison to large bowl; set aside while you brown the remaining venison cubes. Return all venison to Dutch oven.

In small saucepan, heat brandy over low heat until just warm. Remove saucepan from heat and carefully ignite brandy with long-handled match. When flames die out, pour brandy over venison in Dutch oven. Stir in burgundy, broth and bay leaves. Heat to boiling. Reduce heat and simmer, covered, for about 1½ hours. Add mushrooms and simmer for 15 minutes longer. Remove and discard bay leaves. Crumble bacon and add to venison. Serve over hot noodles.

Donna Campopiano, North Scituate, RI

Backstrap and Bacon Rolls

Serves: 8 to 10 ✳ Initial Prep Time: 10 minutes ✳ Marinating Time: 2 hours, or as long as overnight
Prep Time: 35 minutes ✳ Cooking Time: 35 minutes

Fred also prepares this with elk or moose tenderloin, or with boneless duck breasts.

- 3 lbs. venison loin
- ⅔ cup soy sauce
- ⅓ cup Worcestershire sauce
- 1 medium onion
- 1 green bell pepper
- 1 cup whole mushrooms, fresh or canned
- ¾ lb. sliced bacon
- Seasoned salt
- Black pepper
- Cayenne pepper, optional

Cut loin along the length into ¼-inch-thick strips; each strip should be about 1½ inches wide and 10 inches long. Combine soy sauce and Worcestershire sauce in gallon-sized plastic zipper bag. Add venison strips. Seal bag and turn to coat. Refrigerate for 2 to 4 hours, or as long as overnight, turning occasionally.

Prepare hot smoker. Drain marinade into a bowl; set aside. Cut onion, pepper and mushrooms into 1½-inch strips. Lay strips of bacon on work surface. Place a strip of marinated backstrap on top of bacon. Sprinkle with seasoned salt, black pepper and cayenne to taste. Place pieces of onion, bell pepper and mushroom along loin strip, usually 4 or 5 pieces of each. Starting with a short side, roll up tightly jelly-roll-style; the bacon will be on the outside. Secure with wooden toothpicks.

Place rolls on top rack of smoker; do not add any water to the smoker's water pan. Pour half of reserved marinade onto rolls; the marinade should drip into the water pan. Cover smoker and cook for 20 minutes. Turn rolls and douse with remaining marinade. Cook for 15 minutes longer. Bacon should be turning brown on edges. Venison will remain pink in center of roll.

If you prefer, these may be cooked in oven on broiler pan covered with aluminum foil at 350°F for 30 minutes.

Fred B. McCullar, DVM, Water Valley, MS

Venison Mincemeat

Yield: 4 quarts ✳ Prep Time: 20 minutes ✳ Cooking Time: 1 1/2 hours

*A note from Romelle: "This is **real** mincemeat pie—not like the no-meat store types. I usually double the recipe so we can have delicious pies over several months."*

- 2 lbs. boneless cooked venison roast
- 4 lbs. apples, cored and peeled
- 2 lbs. currants and raisins, mixed
- 2 quarts apple cider
- 2 cups packed brown sugar
- 2 cups granulated sugar
- 1 cup molasses
- 2 teaspoons salt
- 1½ teaspoons cinnamon
- ½ teaspoon ground cloves
- ½ teaspoon nutmeg
- ½ teaspoon allspice
- 2 tablespoons lemon juice

Grind venison with meat grinder, or chop to medium-fine consistency in food processor. Transfer venison to nonaluminum Dutch oven. Chop apples; add to venison. Stir in remaining ingredients except lemon juice. Simmer over low heat for about 1½ hours, or until thick. Remove from heat and stir in lemon juice. The mixture may be used immediately, or you may freeze or can it for later use.

To can: Pack hot mixture into hot, sterilized quart jars. Process quarts in pressure cooker for 20 minutes at 15 pounds of pressure; or process for 1 hour and 40 minutes in boiling-water bath.

Kate's note: This is delicious served with dried and fresh fruits, and also makes a nice topping for pancakes, waffles or ice cream.

Romelle Schoff, Unionville, IN

Hungry Hunter's Hotpies

Yield: About 30 hotpies ✳ *Prep Time: 30 minutes* ✳ *Cooking Time: 10 minutes*

Pack some of these in your pocket for your next hunt. Another fun idea is to use a large circle template (like a wide-mouth jar) to cut your circle—then you can make larger hotpies for a main course.

- Half of a medium onion, finely chopped
- 1/2 cup diced celery
- 1 teaspoon vegetable oil
- 1 lb. leftover caribou or other game roast, chilled
- 2 medium potatoes, baked whole and chilled
- 1/2 cup shredded Monterey Jack cheese
- 1 teaspoon crumbled dried thyme
- 1/2 teaspoon salt
- 1/2 teaspoon freshly ground pepper
- 2 eggs, well beaten, divided
- Pastry dough for 2-crust pie
- A little all-purpose flour for rolling out pastry

In small skillet, sauté onion and celery in oil over medium heat until transparent. Transfer to large bowl and set aside to cool. Meanwhile, chop cold roast and potatoes into small dice; add to onion mixture. Stir in cheese, thyme, salt and pepper. Add about half of the eggs to the bowl and mix well. Set aside.

Heat oven to 350°F. Divide pastry dough into 2 portions. Roll out 1 portion on floured surface to 1/4-inch thickness. Using large biscuit cutter or drinking glass dipped in flour, cut pastry into 3-inch circles. Fill each pastry circle with about 1 tablespoon of the filling. Lightly brush edges with reserved egg to help seal the hotpie; crimp edges together with fork. Place on baking sheet. Repeat with remaining ingredients, rolling out second pastry dough when needed. Prick each hotpie with fork to create steam vent; brush tops with remaining egg so they will brown nicely. Bake for about 10 minutes, or until golden brown. Serve hot or at room temperature.

John & Heather Koenig, Concrete, WA

Tracks-in-the-Snow Cacciatore

Serves: 4 to 6 ✳ Prep Time: 10 minutes ✳ Cooking Time: 2 to 3 hours

- 2 lbs. venison stew meat, cut into ¾-inch cubes
- 1 medium onion, chopped
- 1 green bell pepper, chopped
- 2 cloves garlic, crushed
- 3 tablespoons olive oil
- ½ cup dry white wine
- 1 can (14½ oz.) tomatoes, undrained
- 1 can (8 oz.) mushrooms, drained
- 1 teaspoon crumbled dried basil
- 1 teaspoon crumbled dried rosemary
- 1 teaspoon crumbled dried oregano
- Hot cooked rice or noodles for serving

Pat venison dry; set aside. In Dutch oven, sauté onion, pepper and garlic in oil over medium heat until tender. Add venison and cook until browned on all sides. Pour wine over meat and simmer for 3 minutes. Add remaining ingredients except rice. Reduce heat to low; cover and simmer for 2 to 3 hours, or until tender. Serve over rice or noodles.

Kate's note: While canned mushrooms work well here, they usually don't have to cook as long as fresh ones. I chose to add the canned mushrooms during the last 45 minutes of cooking.

R. B. Waddell, Youngstown, NY

Wild Spirit Venison Meatloaf

Serves: 4 to 6 ✳ Prep Time: 20 minutes ✳ Cooking Time: 1 hour

- 2 eggs, lightly beaten
- 1 onion, finely chopped
- 2 cloves garlic, minced
- ⅔ cup bread crumbs
- ⅓ cup packed brown sugar
- ¼ cup milk
- ¼ cup ketchup
- 2 tablespoons prepared horseradish
- 2 tablespoons vinegar
- 2 tablespoons spicy mustard
- 1 teaspoon Worcestershire sauce
- ½ teaspoon salt
- 1½ lbs. ground venison
- 1 cup spaghetti sauce
- 2 tablespoons grated Parmesan cheese

Heat oven to 350°F. Lightly grease loaf pan; set aside. In large bowl, combine all ingredients except ground venison, spaghetti sauce and cheese; mix well. Add ground venison; mix gently but thoroughly. Pack venison mixture into prepared pan. Top with spaghetti sauce; sprinkle with Parmesan cheese. Bake until center reaches 160°F, about 1 hour.

Christopher Hajjar, Pittsfield, MA

Antlered Eggplant Casserole

Serves: 4 to 6 ✳ Prep Time: 10 minutes ✳ Cooking Time: 1¼ hours

- 1½ lbs. ground venison
- 1 medium onion, chopped
- 3 cloves garlic, minced
- 1 large eggplant (about 1½ lbs.), peeled and cubed
- 1 can (28 oz.) crushed tomatoes, undrained
- 1 green bell pepper, diced
- 1 red bell pepper, diced
- ¾ cup seasoned bread crumbs
- 1 teaspoon salt
- 1 teaspoon crumbled dried basil
- ¼ cup grated Parmesan cheese

Heat oven to 350°F. Lightly grease 9x13-inch baking dish; set aside. Heat large nonstick saucepan or Dutch oven over medium heat. Add venison, onion and garlic. Cook until meat is no longer pink and onion is soft, stirring occasionally to break up meat. Add eggplant, tomatoes with juices, green and red bell peppers, bread crumbs, salt and basil; heat to boiling, stirring occasionally. Transfer venison mixture to baking dish. Cover and bake until vegetables are tender, 45 to 50 minutes. Uncover, sprinkle with cheese and bake until cheese is lightly browned, about 15 minutes longer. Let stand for 5 minutes before serving.

Dean & Phyllis Brittenham, Garwin, IN

Game-Care Tips

If you're like me, you may take a look at this section of the cookbook as sort of a refresher course or to see if there's anything "new" in the way of field-dressing game. As old as the sport of hunting is, though, one thing hasn't changed, and that is the fact that any slaughtered animal—be it deer, pig, steer, calf or chicken—must be field-dressed as soon as possible.

Billions of bacteria exist naturally in living carcasses. Once the animal has stopped pumping blood, however, all restraints are let loose. The bacteria have a chance to multiply and will devour the carcass if given time. So, our job is to open up the carcass, get the entrails out as soon as we can and keep the body cavity open, clean and cool.

Ideally, your moose, deer, caribou or elk should be field-dressed within an hour of expiring. Even if it is very cold out, bacteria immediately begin their work in the warm environs of the carcass. Once you locate and tag your trophy (depending upon the area's game laws, you may not have to tag it until you are back at camp), move the carcass to a shady spot if it is a warm day and place the head end slightly uphill.

Field-dressing and dragging will be much easier if you have a hunting buddy with you. If your trophy happens to be a larger member of the deer family, like elk, moose or caribou, and you are alone, you must prepare for the job ahead. Take your time, because the strenuous work is just beginning.

For your first field-dressing step, puncture the hide and cut slightly into the body cavity just below the rib cage and down a few inches toward the anus. This will get at least some of the air out of the cavity and keep it from bloating before you begin field-dressing, and is especially important if you're in a spot where moving around is difficult.

If you are alone, or are waiting for your hunting companion to reach you, do as I've done on many occasions: use natural surroundings to help you out. You might be able to drag your deer

This 1902 photo from *Outdoor Life* magazine shows two well-dressed hunters carrying a good buck. The original photo caption read, "A California hunt—too heavy for one."

so the front end is between two sturdy trees; roll the animal on its back and wrap one leg behind each tree to keep it steady. This will help when you are cutting the hide and removing entrails.

If ticks are prevalent in your hunting area, it's a wise idea to use gutting gloves when field-dressing. These light rubber gloves extend past the elbow and can be secured by a hunting shirt or jacket. This allows you to keep your mind on the job ahead and not on the ticks jumping up off a soon-to-be-cold host to your nice, warm body.

With gloves on and sharp knife in hand, make a circular cut around the anus. Work your knife up inside the cavity, cutting deeply enough to free the intestine from the body cavity wall. Some (I'd like to know just who) have likened this to coring an apple. Next, standing behind the deer with its hind legs propped on either side of you, use the tip of your knife to make a hole in the hide between the hind legs. Slit through the hide all the way up to the hole you punched at the base of the rib cage; if dressing a buck, cut along one side of the external reproductive organs (unless you are thoroughly familiar with the local game laws, it's always a good idea to leave the sex organs attached). If you want a cape for mounting, do not cut any farther up the hide than the hole at the base of the ribs; it's always best to have a little extra cape rather than not enough. Here's a neat little trick Peter taught me years ago. If you come prepared, this step of field-dressing can be made much cleaner and quicker by using a box cutter with a single razor blade. The razor slices quickly through the hide and you can also use it to remove hair that surrounds the incision, making the job less of a hairy mess.

Next, return to the area between the hind legs. Cut into the lining of the body cavity, but not so deep that you puncture any entrails. Use your index and middle fingers on one hand, palm up, as a guide for the knife in your other hand, and cut toward the ribs. The entrails will naturally push out of the opening. Stop again at the bottom of the rib cage.

Return to the pelvis and slice through the center to the pelvic bone. Use a bone saw or whack the back of your hunting knife with a rock to split the pelvic bone open; you will need to use pressure to physically split the legs apart. Once the pelvis is split, use your knife to separate the intestines from the sides of the body cavity and from the wall underneath the pelvic bone. Also separate the diaphragm from the ribs and the spine. Carefully reach up as far as you can into the throat area— as high as your arms will take you—to sever the esophagus and trachea. Be aware of where your knife is, as most knife accidents occur during this step where you can't see what you're cutting.

Once all the entrails have been separated from the body cavity, they will simply pour out to one side. If you want to save the heart or liver and can readily pick it out of the entrails, remove them before you tip out the guts. This way they won't get dirty with leaves and twigs. Place them in a plastic bag or double-wrap in cheesecloth. These, too, should be allowed to cool.

If you are alone, turn the animal on its side, or, if you're with a hunting buddy, lift up the forequarters of the animal and turn to one side to dump out the entrails. Then, move the animal away from the entrails and roll it over on its belly to drain any remaining blood. If you can, pull it farther up hill to aid in drainage. If you will be leaving to get help before dragging the deer out, move the carcass to a shady spot and prop the body cavity open with a stick; or, even better, hang it from a tree in a shady spot.

There are several modes of transportation for your game. Most often you'll have to drag the animal to some point where you can load it onto an ATV, truck, car or boat. If you've harvested a bigger member of the deer family, like a moose, elk or caribou, then you're probably going to quarter it in the field and pack out the quarters. Whichever method you choose, keep the meat cool and clean. If you get to a point where it will be transported out in the open and subject to vehicle fumes and dirt, then wrap the carcass in a large mesh or cheesecloth bag. You'll want to keep air circulating, but prevent dirt from getting on the carcass.

Back at camp or home, hang the carcass to further aid in the draining of blood; if possible, wash out the body cavity with cool water. Some hunters prefer to hang the carcass by the head, while others hang by the hind legs so the head is down. Proponents of the head-down theory say that the blood drains more quickly in this position, and that since heat rises, the carcass will cool more rapidly because heat won't be trapped in the chest cavity. Hanging head-down also allows for easier skinning and caping out the hide around the skull.

True aging of meat only occurs under controlled conditions, at a temperature between 32°F and 38°F. If you do not have a controlled environment, then whatever extra time the carcass spends hanging before it is butchered is not truly "aging." Should you have a foolproof method of hanging deer for a few days, stick with it. But, if this is new to you, I advise getting your venison butchered as soon as possible. I like to butcher, wrap and freeze my venison within a few days of shooting the deer.

Here's a tip once you have skinned the carcass. While the carcass is still hanging, use a small propane torch to gently singe any leftover deer hair. It'll be well worth the few extra minutes to remove the annoying hair and will not hurt the meat in any manner as long as it is done properly.

Butchering is a key step in processing venison. Entire books have been written on this subject alone, and I won't go into that here. I recommend that you get your meat butchered professionally. When you take your deer to a butcher for processing, be sure to discuss how you want the meat cut up and wrapped. Keep in mind that it's better to freeze venison in larger pieces rather than smaller ones. For instance, even though loins can be used for medallions, keep them whole until you are ready to prepare your entrée.

I like to have most of my meat frozen in meal-sized portions. For example, all our ground venison is packaged in 1½- to 2-pound packages. Since I am often cooking for the three of us, this is a good size for most of my recipes. If you have a larger family, freeze your meat in portions that you would use in one meal.

Proper labeling is a must. The butcher should have marked each package as to the type of cut, but you should take it a step further before storing the meat in the freezer. Since flavor can vary from animal to animal, even in the same species, it's a good idea to be detailed in your labeling. This past season was a busy one for Peter and me. We were fortunate enough to bring home caribou and black bear from northern Quebec, moose from northern Newfoundland, and deer from both Michigan and New York. We decided on a coding system that labeled each piece of wrapped meat with the species, where it came from and the year. For example, a package of ground venison from the New York buck was labeled, "Ground/D/NY-00" and stew meat from the caribou was labeled, "Stew/C/Q-00." This way, there's no need to wonder what to expect when pulling venison from the freezer.

Meat from the butcher will probably be wrapped in freezer paper. I always place this wrapped package in a zippered plastic freezer bag. If you do this, be sure to squeeze the bag as you seal it to remove as much air as possible.

I like to save out a few choice cuts right after the butchering is done, to enjoy right away, before freezing the rest. Remember, too, that the longer you leave the meat in the freezer, the greater the

Butchering your own deer

If you do decide to butcher your own deer, keep your work area as clean as possible. Meat is highly perishable and can be contaminated by a dirty work surface, dirty knives, and bacteria from humans as well as other animals (or critters) in the work environment.

Follow the recommendations in the text for portioning and package size. Also, when you freeze large, whole portions of meat, leave a bit of the fat and connective tissue on the roast to help protect the meat from freezer burn. Trim the meat well before cooking; it is often easier to trim a piece of venison when it is still slightly frozen.

For optimum results, use a vacuum sealer to remove all air from packages before freezing. This completely eliminates the chance of freezer burn. Many vacuum sealers are available for home use that aren't too expensive. But, when I went to purchase mine, I decided on the unit that was a little more expensive because I thought the extra money would well outweigh the downside of freezer burn!

If a vacuum sealer is not in your kitchen, wrap the meat in a layer of a good plastic wrap, such as Saran. Press the wrap close to the meat to push out all air and eliminate air pockets. If you are freezing a tied roast, be sure that it has been tied tightly to eliminate internal air pockets.

Once the meat has been wrapped in plastic, wrap it in freezer paper. Often referred to as butcher paper, this special wrap is plastic-coated on one side. Tear off a sheet that is at least twice the size of the meat. Bring two opposite side edges together on top of the meat. Start folding in one-inch folds until the paper is against the meat. Turn the meat over and fold the other ends toward the meat, squeezing out any air. Secure the ends with tape.

Finally, label the package as noted in the text; for extra protection, place the paper-wrapped parcel into a freezer bag as described. Freeze in the coldest part of the freezer, keeping the packages in a single layer if possible until the meat is completely frozen.

chance for freezer burn, which is the biggest cause of flavor loss in my opinion.

Well, you've had a successful hunt and have properly taken care of getting your prized venison to the freezer to enjoy for many months to come. Here are some tips on enjoying your venison from the freezer.

One of my favorite courses while at Cornell University's Hotel School was Microbiology (or Sanitation, as it was named in my day). Mrs. Bonnie Richmond taught students all the whys and wherefores of bacterial growth in and out of the kitchen. This was fascinating to me, and carried over into my favorite occupation of cooking venison. I think you'll enjoy the bit of detailed information that follows.

To give your venison the proper respect for all the time you put into proper field care, the right butchering, meticulous wrapping, labeling and freezing, make sure you thaw your venison properly, too. Be sure that the meat is completely thawed before you cook it. If you cook partially frozen meats you will run into complications. A roast may be cooked on the outside and still raw on the inside. Also, cooking time may be increased by as much as threefold if the roast is not completely thawed. If you brown ground venison from the frozen state, the meat on the outside will be overcooked by the time the ground venison from the frozen center is cooked. In contrast, cooking completely thawed meat that was properly frozen to begin with is like cooking fresh meat.

The best way to thaw venison is in the refrigerator. A great tip for tastier venison is to place the meat on a rack, which will allow excess blood to drain while the meat is defrosting. Depending upon the size of the piece of meat and the temperature setting of your refrigerator, thawing may take 12 hours to a day or even longer. We keep a very cold refrigerator; in fact, it's so cold that ice crystals form in our containers of iced tea and orange juice. So, most of my venison needs at least a day to defrost.

The second-best method for thawing frozen meat is under cool running water from the faucet. This will warm up the frozen meat, yet not bring it up to a temperature where bacterial growth can begin. Thawing venison under running water will speed up the thawing process compared to the refrigerator, but is sometimes impractical where water supplies aren't always plentiful.

Having grown up in the East, where water is taken for granted, I first learned about "water shares" out west from Peter. When he lived in southern Colorado, he had a small ranch with water shares. On certain days of the week, the water was diverted for his use, so he would fill up his cistern and water the horses. On other days, the water was diverted for the neighboring ranch. So, I can imagine that in places like this, leaving a faucet open with running water for an hour or more is not practical. In fact, the only other place I've seen this method employed is in cooking schools, commercial kitchens or in restaurants.

The last method, and least preferred, is to thaw meats at room temperature. This is a risky venture. Thawing meats at room temperature always permits bacterial growth to occur at a rapid rate. Bacteria love to multiply at temperatures between 45°F and 140°F. I don't think any of us have kitchens that fall outside of this range. Keeping venison below 45°F while defrosting will inhibit bacterial growth. The bacteria can still multiply, however, because the only way to kill most disease-causing bacteria is to subject them to temperatures above 170°F for a short period of time (about 30 seconds).

While bacterial growth will occur on the outside surfaces of steaks, chops, ribs and loin portions, most of the bacteria is eliminated during cooking if the outside surfaces are seared or grilled at temperatures above 170°F. However, it is the ground meat and rolled roasts that are of greatest concern. Because the meat in the center of a package of ground venison has already been subject to air and possible contaminants, it is highly susceptible to bacterial spoilage if left at room temperature to thaw; and this is of particular concern if the final cooking procedure does not bring the temperature of the meat to 170°F. Roasts that have been rolled and tied prior to freezing have been subject to air and possible contaminants as well. If you follow the general guidelines of pulling a roast from the oven when it has reached an internal temperature of 125° to 130°F, there may still be bacteria in the center of the roast. My universal recommendation, therefore, is to thaw venison in the refrigerator, not at room temperature.

Some of you may ask, why not thaw venison in the microwave? I've experimented with this technique on and off over the years. I've used small wrapped and unwrapped cuts, larger pieces under "lower" powers, smaller microwave ovens and larger microwave ovens, and still have not yet found a happy solution to thawing venison in a microwave. The basis of microwave cooking is that the radiation generated by the oven penetrates the meat and agitates the water molecules. When the water molecules start moving around a lot, this generates heat which, in turn, thaws the meat. But, since most microwave radiation only reaches about two inches into foods, the heat can only reach further into the product after the outer portion is already much warmer. This is why most meats will brown on the outside yet remain raw on the inside when defrosted in the microwave. In addition, because venison is so lean, the meat fibers tend to shrink and lose moisture. Venison can't afford to lose moisture. Even cuts like stew meat become tougher because the connective tissues and elastin shrink and become firmer. (Remember that stew meats must be cooked with moist heat methods to break down the connective tissue.) While using a microwave to defrost venison meat may save time, it will cost you flavor.

When we buy meat at the supermarket, we have no way of knowing what type of animal the meat came from, how it was processed or how it was handled before reaching the supermarket meat case. With our own game meat, we have control over what happens to the meat before it reaches the table. By following proper field-care procedures, and handling the meat meticulously in all steps from butchering, wrapping and freezing to thawing and cooking, you will be able to serve venison meals that are truly "fit for a king."

Nutritional Information

If a recipe has a range of servings, the data below applies to the greater number of servings. If the recipe lists a quantity range for an ingredient, the average quantity was used to calculate the nutritional data. In recipes that call for "vension" without specifying what type, deer venison was assumed. If alternate ingredients are listed, the analysis applies to the first ingredient, with one exception: beef gravy was used in place of brown sauce. Low-sodium soy sauce was assumed in recipes that call for soy sauce. Sauces are not included in the analysis if they are listed in finished form in the ingredients list (such as "Horseradish Cream Sauce, p. 82"). Optional ingredients and ingredients listed as serving suggestions (such as "hot cooked rice") are also not included in the analysis.

	Calories	Protein (g)	Fat (g)	Saturated Fat (g)	Carbohydrate (g)	Sodium (mg)	Cholesterol (mg)
Starters							
Far East Venison Fondue	229	26	12	2	2	263	96
Mushrooms with Venison Stuffing	97	5	6	3	6	201	17
San Antonio Venison Cabbage Dip	373	12	31	12	11	658	59
South-of-the-Border Venison Dip	236	11	15	9	14	452	46
Svenska Venison Meatball Picks	319	13	28	15	5	304	130
Sweet Cherry Peppers with Venison Stuffing	187	6	13	3	10	765	17
Tender Venison Finger Rolls	575	37	27	5	43	1092	156
Tex-Mex Egg Rolls (2)	468	20	25	9	40	561	66
Venison Carpaccio with Mustard Sauce	411	13	38	6	2	602	56
Venison Chili Dip	211	11	15	8	7	403	46
Venison Pulgogi	152	17	6	1	7	426	60
Venison Terrine	220	33	7	2	4	88	116
Main Meals							
Adirondack Spinach Venison Roast	449	50	24	13	6	259	207
Applejack Venison Medallions	444	27	35	21	2	525	195
Baked Moose Ale Ribs	310	34	1	>1	41	384	88
Blackened Cajun Medallions of Venison	263	33	12	7	4	394	144
Broccoli-Venison Stir-Fry	452	33	31	6	12	826	96
Canadian Barren-Ground Caribou Tenderloin	1214	45	94	45	36	161	366
Chicken-Fried Venison	407	41	17	4	21	324	175
Chinese Vension Steak with Mushrooms	290	29	14	3	11	251	96
Christmas Venison Roast with Baby Mushrooms	529	53	28	16	9	712	216
Curry Grilled Venison Steaks	207	39	4	2	1	1235	143
Grilled Elk Steak Florentine	696	85	33	6	16	3295	186
Grilled Moose Burgers	368	45	10	3	22	531	111
Grilled Stuffed Venison Burgers	625	50	43	21	5	909	218
Gunnison Venison Goulash	327	37	15	4	11	100	137
Hunter's Venison Stroganoff	392	35	20	8	15	301	129
Meatloaf Parmentier	417	26	24	11	23	451	155
New Year's Eve Rack of Venison Ribs	794	57	51	30	23	601	354

	Calories	Protein (g)	Fat (g)	Saturated Fat (g)	Carbohydrate (g)	Sodium (mg)	Cholesterol (mg)
Main Meals (cont.)							
Pan-Fried Venison with Creamy Peppercorn Sauce	522	43	30	16	19	186	226
Roast Mustard Loin of Venison	416	40	24	4	3	752	145
Roast Venison with Green Peppercorn Sauce	376	40	22	11	2	494	190
Sausage and Peppers Skillet	536	22	37	13	29	411	100
Savory Doe Burgers	650	51	48	23	1	1000	226
Sicilian Venison Burgers	546	35	39	16	14	465	145
Spit-Roasted Leg of Venison	352	56	12	6	2	166	222
Steak au Poivre	381	41	19	9	6	487	186
Steak with Caper-Mustard Sauce	376	43	11	2	22	685	145
Sweet Moose Loin Roast	166	28	3	<1	5	139	76
Thai Marinated Venison Ribbons	403	32	18	6	28	666	96
"Too Late" Venison Cutlet Gruyère	1001	83	46	17	60	2128	329
Venetian Venison Pizza Pie	502	23	30	11	36	1150	73
Venison and Vegetable Kabobs	563	35	41	6	14	1093	119
Venison Bolognese Sauce	501	26	34	13	26	1293	101
Venison Chili Tostadas	390	23	23	9	24	417	84
Venison Cutlet Delight	779	60	43	14	36	1055	254
Venison Filet Wellington	501	39	30	9	17	249	172
Venison Lasagna de Katarina	594	33	33	16	40	539	111
Venison Medallions with Herbed Cheese Sauce	1241	71	79	43	51	528	409
Venison Parmigiana	1027	83	49	19	62	3361	317
Venison Sausage (1 oz.)	96	5	8	3	<1	100	25
Venison Steak Fajitas	492	49	10	3	50	936	154
Venison Steak Forrestiere	324	37	11	3	14	305	127
Venison Steak Heroes	398	33	8	2	45	932	96
Venison Steak with Red Currants	576	54	24	10	31	388	229
Venison-Stuffed Cabbage	414	24	28	14	17	426	114
Venison Tenderloin Siciliano	426	32	18	6	26	594	115
Western Style Bar-B-Que Venison Chops	204	39	4	2	1	69	143
Wild Game Lasagna Italiano	532	23	26	12	52	743	75

	Calories	Protein (g)	Fat (g)	Saturated Fat (g)	Carbohydrate (g)	Sodium (mg)	Cholesterol (mg)
Venison for Breakfast							
Simple Venison Omelet	636	36	53	25	2	547	552
Venison Asparagus Delight	742	55	56	27	3	685	652
Venison Vegetable Frittata	349	24	25	11	8	330	343
Pies and Casseroles							
Baked Ziti with Venison	816	46	46	21	54	1245	154
Chili Casserole	583	32	37	16	31	915	117
Deer Camp Casserole	685	27	49	22	34	766	127
Eggplant-Venison Casserole	547	35	38	18	18	825	150
Leftover Venison Pot Pie	683	46	33	10	50	1065	142
Quick Venison Chili Pie	459	25	32	14	18	650	164
Venison Moussaka	765	28	61	28	27	982	268
Venison Tamale Pie	654	30	44	19	36	933	146
Venison-Barley Casserole	623	32	28	12	64	1111	103
Soups, Stews and Chilies							
Escarole Soup with Venison Meat-a-Balls	377	21	27	10	12	1320	107
It's a Meal Venison Soup	255	26	5	1	26	585	80
Kate's Triple-K Chili	409	27	24	11	22	783	101
November Venison Stew	234	28	6	2	15	465	96
Quickie Venison Chili	431	27	27	11	20	945	101
Slow-Cooker Chili	296	19	13	6	28	350	51
Venison Meatball Stew	565	31	32	13	41	2120	154
Venison Minestrone Soup	273	21	6	1	34	1248	50
Venison Onion Soup	455	39	13	2	46	800	117
Venison Stew with Barley	453	47	9	2	47	714	147
Warwick Venison Stew	226	29	6	2	14	240	99
Marinades, Rubs, Butters and Sauces							
Béchamel Sauce (1/4 c.)	98	3	7	4	6	31	22
Chimayo Chile Sauce (1/4 c.)	135	2	9	1	12	188	0
Garlic Butter (1 T.)	106	<1	12	7	1	74	31
Garlic Sauce (1 T.)	91	<1	9	1	2	67	<1
Herbed Butter (1 T.)	102	<1	11	7	<1	2	31
Horseradish Cream Sauce (1 T.)	53	<1	6	3	1	24	20
Hunter's Sauce (1/4 c.)	86	2	6	3	6	227	12
Mustard Sauce (1 T.)	40	<1	4	2	<1	42	6
Peppered Butter (1 T.)	102	<1	12	7	<1	146	31
Red Wine Marinade (1/4 c.)	86	<1	7	<1	6	132	0
Sesame Ginger Marinade (1/4 c.)	200	2	18	2	9	607	0
Simple Marinade (1/4 c.)	390	<1	43	6	2	3	0
South-of-the-Border BBQ Rub (1/4 c.)	97	3	2	<1	22	1786	0
Spicy Beer Marinade (1/4 c.)	79	<1	<1	0	21	153	0

	Calories	Protein (g)	Fat (g)	Saturated Fat (g)	Carbohydrate (g)	Sodium (mg)	Cholesterol (mg)
Marinades, Rubs, Butters and Sauces (cont.)							
Spicy Far East Dipping Sauce (1 T.)	40	<1	4	1	1	258	0
Tomato Butter (1 T.)	103	<1	12	7	<1	2	31
Tri-Color Peppercorn Rub (1 tsp.)	7	<1	<1	0	1	62	0
Wasabi Rub (1 T.)	20	1	<1	0	3	151	0
Game Accompaniments							
Broccoli Casserole	252	11	21	12	5	379	166
Brown Rice Salad	248	5	11	1	35	399	2
Cheesy Garlic Mashed Potatoes	320	7	22	14	26	395	66
Corn Relish	229	1	18	1	17	473	0
Fusilli Salad	489	12	21	3	64	373	1
Pungent Caramelized Onions	100	2	6	1	12	100	0
Roasted Herbed New Potatoes	238	3	15	5	24	213	16
Rummied Sweet Potato Casserole	585	6	14	8	113	171	31
Summertime Vegetable Pie	311	16	21	7	16	387	136
Super Herbed Italian Bread	304	6	21	8	24	496	34
Wild Rice Casserole	159	5	6	3	23	720	10
Premier Wild Chefs							
Anticosti Outfitters Braised Deer	225	35	7	3	3	203	137
Cedar Ridge Outfitters Red Stroganoff	279	38	8	2	14	1218	116
Conklin's Lodge Venison Roll-Ups	182	25	8	3	<1	249	88
Legends Ranch Herbed Venison Rolls	536	47	20	11	38	1430	308
Lucky Star Ranch Venison Stew	517	40	23	12	37	521	188
Midwest Venison Casserole	635	27	37	15	48	1997	95
Sun Canyon Ranch Crock-Pot Pepper Steak	251	29	7	1	19	541	96
Tuckamore Lodge Salisbury Moose Steak with Mushroom Sauce	435	24	30	15	16	1092	117
Whale River Lodge Caribou Stroganoff	456	53	20	10	13	840	217
Your Best Recipes							
"1000-Year-Old" Stew	540	49	16	3	51	228	129
Antlered Eggplant Casserole	437	28	25	12	27	1116	104
Backstrap and Bacon Rolls	242	36	8	3	5	1142	124
Boneless Roast with Creamy Peppercorn Sauce	234	34	6	3	5	601	131
Down-Home Jerky (1 slice)	26	4	<1	<1	1	90	16
Grilled Peppered Venison Loin with Portobello Sauce	489	49	22	10	25	756	175
Hungry Hunter's Hotpies	117	6	6	2	10	127	33
"Refrigerator-Smoked" Venison Ham	319	53	6	2	11	284	190
Tangy Venison Stew	348	33	8	2	36	653	98
Tracks-in-the-Snow Cacciatore	280	36	11	2	8	291	129
Venison Bourguignon	427	41	25	5	8	852	153
Venison Mincemeat (1/4 c.)	151	4	<1	<1	35	87	12
Wild Spirit Venison Meatloaf	510	27	29	13	34	806	175

Mail-Order Sources

Broadleaf Venison USA, Inc.
3050 East 11th Street
Los Angeles, CA 90023
800-336-3844
www.broadleafgame.com
venison, buffalo, wild boar, elk, rattlesnake, rabbit, ostrich,
lamb, alligator, kangaroo, game birds and gourmet ravioli

Broken Arrow Ranch
P.O. Box 530
Ingram, TX 78025
800-962-4263
www.brokenarrowranch.com
venison, antelope, wild boar and game sausages, stews
and chilies

D'Artagnan Inc.
399 St. Paul Avenue
Jersey City, NJ 07306
800-DARTAGNAN
www.dartagnan.com
venison, buffalo, duck, game birds, ostrich, pheasant, rabbit,
wild mushrooms, truffles and pâtés

Durham Meat Company
P.O. Box 26158
San Jose, CA 95159
800-233-8742
www.durhammeat.com
venison, buffalo, wild boar, caribou, antelope, alligator,
kangaroo, rattlesnake, ostrich, turtle, frog legs, small
game and wild game sausages

The Game Exchange (Polarica)
P.O. Box 990204
San Francisco, CA 94124
800-GAME-USA
www.polarica.com
venison, caribou, elk, buffalo, antelope, wild boar, rabbit,
rattlesnake, turtle, frog legs, alligator, ostrich, kangaroo,
wild mushrooms, pâtés and game sausages

Game Sales International
2456 E. 13th Street
P.O. Box 7719
Loveland, CO 80537
800-729-2090
www.gamesalesintl.com
venison, buffalo, caribou, elk, boar, muskox, turtle, alligator, frog legs, rabbit, ostrich, kangaroo, gourmet spices,
flavorings, oils, wild mushrooms, fruit and rice

Hills Food Ltd.
#109-3650 Bonneville Place
Burnaby, British Columbia
Canada V3N 4T7
604-421-3100
hillsfood@bc.sympatico.ca
NOTE: wholesale distributors only
www.hillsfoods.com
venison, elk, caribou, bison, muskox, wild boar, pheasant,
quail, ostrich, goose, alligator, rattlesnake, frog, turtle,
wild sea asparagus, fiddleheads and jams

Lofton Ridge Deer and Bison Farm
24740 Lofton Avenue
Chisago City, MN 55013
651-257-8638
venison, elk, bison, boar, turkey, rabbit, foie gras, and magret

Musicon Farms
385 Scotchtown Road
Goshen, NY 10924
845-294-6378
www.koshervenison.com
glatt kosher venison

Native Game
308 Walnut
Brighton, CO 80601
800-952-6321
NOTE: wholesale distributors only
www.nativegame.bigstep.com
buffalo, elk, caribou, venison, antelope, alligator, rattlesnake, game sausages, game birds, bear, kangaroo,
ostrich, and other exotic and African game

Nicky USA, Inc.
223 S.E. 3rd Avenue
Portland, OR 97214
800-469-4162
www.nickyusawildgame.com
venison, elk, boar, bison, duck, partridge, pheasant, antelope,
caribou, muskox, alligator, frog legs, turtle, rattlesnake,
kangaroo, emu, ostrich, sausages, pâtés, wild mushrooms, huckleberries, fiddleheads and truffles

Nightbird
358 Shaw Road
South San Francisco, CA 94080
800-225-7457
venison, buffalo, wild boar, caribou, antelope, alligator,
kangaroo, rattlesnake, ostrich, turtle, frog legs, small
game and wild game sausages

Prairie Harvest
P.O. Box 1013
Spearfish, SD 57783
800-350-7166
www.prairieharvest.com
venison, bear, buffalo, caribou, elk, boar, muskox, ostrich,
turtle, alligator, frog legs, small game and other wild game
sausages

The Sausage Maker Inc.
1500 Clinton Street, Bldg 123
Buffalo, NY 14206
716-824-6510
www.sausagemaker.com
everything you need for making sausage: seasonings, spices,
stuffers, casings, scales, smokehouses, grills, grinders, cut-
lery, dehydrators, thermometers, food processing and pre-
serving equipment, and sausage-making kits

Shaffer Venison Farms, Inc.
RR 1 Box 172
Herndon PA 17830
Phone: 1-800-446-3745
Fax: 570-758-4476
www.shafferfarms.com
venison and deer skin products

Specialty World Foods
84 Montgomery Street
Albany, NY 12207
800-233-0193
venison, buffalo, caribou, elk, boar, muskox, turtle, alligator,
frog legs, rabbit, ostrich, kangaroo, and a host of other specialty foods including wild game raviolis and wild game sausage

Index

Creative Publishing international, Inc.
offers a variety of how-to books.

For information call or write:
Creative Publishing international, Inc.
Subscriber Books
5900 Green Oak Drive
Minnetonka, MN 55343
1-800-328-3895

Or visit us at:
www.howtobookstore.com